Bigger Than Me

An Untold Story of Sex and Love Addiction

Ryan Capitol

*Our mission is to efficiently provide the world's finest, most comprehensive
book publishing service, enabling every author to experience success.
To find out how to publish your book, your way, and have it available
worldwide, visit us online at www.trafford.com*

Trafford rev. 7/21/2010

 www.trafford.com

North America & international
toll-free: 1 888 232 4444 (USA & Canada)
phone: 250 383 6864 ♦ fax: 812 355 4082

Chapter 1

THE BEGINNINGS OF ADDICTION

When I tell people my story about how I became addicted to sex and love, I tell them it started at about the age of four, but in reality it started even before I was born. This was only where my history started in the line of things. The actual history behind my behavior actually goes back several generations. My addictive behavior is one that is a family secret that only until the truth of the matter is told, wills a cure be foreseen.

For a long time I had the idea that I was the only one who had this problem. That turned out to be a false accusation. In today's society, times are changing for addictive behaviors, doctors and medicines are being developed for people, to help them fight the urge to have sexual compulsive behaviors. I am not a doctor, but I am an addict, and believe me those medicines work very well. But again this book isn't about getting help anymore than Dr. Patrick Carnes' book

"Out of the Shadows" which describes many areas of sexual addiction and love addiction. I would suggest that anyone who feels that they have a problem with sexual compulsive behaviors to read this book and even more I would suggest this book for any of those people who are having the feelings of a significant other who is controlling in bed, or if that same person spends more time alone than with others, that "Out of the Shadows" is probably for you.

This story is about how my addiction started, how it progressed, and how it unleashed me into a world I couldn't have known existed had it not been for those people who truly loved me. I know now that I wouldn't have survived had it not been for love. Even though I was addicted to love, affection, and intimacy, I couldn't begin to know what love was until I was shown it outside of my family. I couldn't see love as anything but sex and intercourse with another human being. That is what this story is about. This story is about the human factor of my addiction and how it started for me.

I can't speak for anyone else's beginning of addictive sexual behavior because everyone else is different from my story. Most of the time it only takes one event of another person to awaken sexual awareness and impurity. I can sympathize with every one of their stories, however. And I know that everyone of them including myself has suffered the same fate as the ones we have harmed, if not worse than how we harmed others. It is only a part of our reasoning to show affection towards those whom we feel attractions to. For me it was women in general.

My story started with my family. My brother was just starting junior high school. I didn't even care what school was at this point in time. I wanted to just be able to go to and meet other kids my age. My grandmother and my father's brother would take care of me until my brother got out of school. My brother would then escort me to our home three blocks away.

As any child that was much younger than their older sibling, I found myself constantly wanting to be around my big brother for the idea that he could teach me things that my parents couldn't. I would hang out with him all day long if I could in those days.

He would be doing homework or talking on the phone to one of his friends. I of course would get on another phone to listen in on the conversation. Occasionally I would giggle and tell stories that would embarrass him in front of his girlfriends. He of course didn't like his privacy broken by anyone, especially a four-year-old boy who didn't know a thing about privacy.

That is when the violence would start. It was a cat and mouse game where my brother would hunt me down and unleash his wrath upon my body. He would chase me down, pin my hands under his knees, and then tickle me until my face turned purple. He covered my mouth and tickled me even more depending on if anyone could hear my screams. As the tears rolled down my face from the beating of sorts, he would tell me to stop crying, grow up, and if I didn't stop crying he would do it even longer the next time.

I learned quickly that bothering him in any situation especially on the phone caused him to go off on a tantrum of a rage. He took it out on me of course. And eventually he came up with newer ways to punish me. He invented the gay cowboy known as "Rump Ranger." The ranger was mean and took over my brother's body with a very scary vengeance on my buttocks. My brother was no longer at home inside of his body. Inside of my body I found out the reason for the name of "Rump Ranger." It was because my brother used his penis to rape his victims in the rectum and force me to suck his penis.

Instead of just tickling me he added oral sex and anal sex to the torture on almost a daily basis. He was performing as the "Rump Ranger" as much as he could just to humiliate me further from being around him. The pain was excruciating at first, but I managed to get used to it over time. He would eventually start doing it while my parents were in their bedroom next to his room. They would walk right by as I was under the covers sucking on my brother's penis. Many times my parents thought that we were horsing around and my brother would tell me that he would kill me in my sleep if I told anyone. I was a very good daydreamer after that day. I also became very adamant about playing hide and go seek. I would hide in places where my brother wouldn't find me at all. I felt I was an expert at the birds and bees by age five.

I remember the first baby sitter that I had because they reminded me of my favorite cartoon characters, "Tom & Jerry". The two had names that rhymed with that title so I would constantly have a problem with their names. I always was amazed at the way the wife of the couple would be working out while she watched over various children. I had one really good friend and amazingly it was a girl. She treated me with respect. I felt I was normal around her, and not something to beat up and push around. She made it easy for me to like being around girls along with the help of the babysitter. My parents said I had a crush on her. I didn't believe that, but they said I didn't want to leave her side as a child. Today I look back at that event and say "duh!"

The way that she treated me was like a magic show and we were the stars of the program. She was the queen and I was her king. I felt like she could save me from the problems I had at home daily with my older brother. That girl and I were inseparable. We were connected at the hip, and we galloped throughout the day together until she started kindergarten. For some reason I had to go there too. She went to the same school as I did, but she wasn't about to be seen around other boys, but I was different at first. I didn't act like other boys. I was cool and accepted everyone.

That acceptance of everyone would later get me into a huge falling out between all of the girls I had come to know. Boys weren't supposed to like girls. Girls had coodies, and girls drooled, according to other boys. I told the boys who were saying these cruel things about girls that they didn't know what they were talking about. Girls are awesome and they complete us as boys. No one would listen to my words. I eventually accepted it when my best friend betrayed me by kicking me to the dirt one day during recess. I cried and asked to go home sick, as I didn't feel good after loosing my best friend to some totally mean people.

I quickly got over her and moved on. I stayed friends with my other comrades and they were a little out-of-place, but I was still cool with most of the other kids at that time. I found out that the reason she didn't like me anymore was because I had to wear glasses. I hated wearing them. My glasses although would help me see the world, couldn't help me see the loving people I once saw without them. I remained cool until my first grade year.

That year I met someone who would change the way I looked at life altogether. This person was quite possibly a third or fourth grade student. He was taller than all of the other kids, he was heavy-set, and his head was shaved. The other children were mocking him, throwing food at him, and teasing him about his height and weight. I put a very abrupt stop to it by stepping in the middle of the food fight that he was being forced to endure. I screamed at the other kids telling them to stop what they were doing and leave him alone. He is probably a nice person. Then I was caught off guard by the school principal. She said I was brave and that I needed to escort the other boy out of the lunchroom and help him get to the class he was in on time. He was a new student at the school and this was his second or third day.

The giant boy stood about four-feet, and I was only about three-foot-nine inches tall. He towered over most of the other kids in our class. I found out that he was in the first grade class with me. I couldn't understand why anyone would take good food and chuck it at such a nice person like him. He didn't even through things back. He just kept eating. He kept complaining about how he didn't want to come back here again the next day. I told him that he was there because he had a purpose. Of course, I was the one really with the purpose for him. He was big and burly and could beat up my brother potentially. Although I wasn't thinking of how quiet, lonely, or scared he was when the other kids were throwing food at him and called him gross. While he was much uncoordinated in his movements, he had a special kind of aura about him that sent me to be near him further on in life.

From that day on, my popularity status dwindled to a flat zero along with my newfound friend's status. He was almost as dumb as a box of rocks, by some people's standards, but occasionally he came back with good remarks, comments, or the unusual smart-assed remarks. I asked him why would he allow those people drag him down like that, and his reply was, "I just don't care about what people think of me!" Which was a lie I found out about later, but he continued; "Besides they are the ones wasting food." "No argument there!" I replied with a laugh. I eventually invited him over to play at my house, but his father wanted to meet up with my parents before they would allow anyone be around his son for extended periods of time. So we set up a time where both of our families could meet each other and begin to get to know one another's families.

When the two families met they hit it off between both sets of parents. My mom and dad were speaking with his mom and dad, and the kids sat around and played games and played with G.I. Joe toys. My new friend and I drew very close and I wanted him around all of the time. That way my brother couldn't hurt me, or so I thought.

The abuse continued to worsen, and my brother's favorite thing after I started bringing over my friends was to torture them as well as me. It was even more humiliating as my older brother would hit, kick, and bite my friends until they wanted to go home. Then he would focus even more on me once they had left the house. What I felt could have been my hope and savior ended up worsening the blow to my credibility as a friend to those closest to me.

I started daydreaming more in class. I dreamt that someone would come by and kidnap me. I never thought I would like going back home each day. But I started going to my dad's mother's house and being watched by my youngest uncle. It was there that the abuse was likable and fun for me. My cousins, who lived with my grandmother at that time, were there, and my oldest girl cousin would treat me nicely, and give me oral sex instead of the other way around. Plus she had holes where my brother didn't and she would allow me to go into those places and it really felt good to do that at first. But how did this happen with all of the adult supervision around. It happened at night.

On many occasions I would stay the night at my grandmother's house where my cousins were staying as well. We would all be sleeping in the same bed as the girls. I found myself attracted to girls and not boys; so being in bed with my female cousins was a plus. I found myself sleeping better after my cousin did things to me like my brother did. Her body parts just seemed much gentler to handle than my brother's parts were. Many nights I would wake up to seeing her on my body naked head-to-toe, making love to my baby-styled twig of a penis. I enjoyed her company, and I never wanted it to stop with her like I did with my brother.

Her loving fashion took my mind away from the pain that my brother forced on me. The love that she had shown towards me silenced his violent rage and outbursts of hatred. I began liking to go to my grandmother's house more than my own. That is until my cousins and their parents had to move to California, where her dad was stationed. Getting rid of the one thing that I loved to hold on to seemed cruel at the time, but I knew that it had to end at some point. I had to attend school. My cousin was in the fourth grade that year and I was in the first grade.

My cousins and sex were all I could think about in class that year. I would daydream in class about sex. I dreamed, daily, about all of the girls in my class that I wanted to have sex with. I drew pictures of how I would have sex with each girl. Eventually the teacher caught me drawing pictures of the events in my mind. It was a good thing that I wasn't a good drawer. I quickly covered my steps by scribbling on the page blacking out the sexual parts. I then proceeded to lie about the way items were drawn. I would make the excuse of a girls name on the page was pure coincidence, and that the girl's name on the page was my cousin's. I claimed that I had new bunk-beds that I wanted to draw. I wanted to invite my cousin's over to see them. I guess I was a better drawer than I thought because my parents were called in to show the sexual scene that I had drawn out on the piece of paper.

Their faces were like blank slates of paper. Their jaws dropped to the floor as they saw I had drawn a girl that was in my class sitting next to me on what I fixed to be bunk-beds. The questions were flying right at my face. They were asking me things like, "Why would you draw something like this?" "Who showed you how to draw this type of picture." And "Why is this girl's name written on the page with an arrow pointing at the girl in the picture?" I don't know how I managed to get out of that classroom filled with such reputation damaging questions. I don't even remember doing any homework, but I do remember my desk being filled with papers that the teacher had given to me. I had assignments that were kept hidden from everyone's view inside of that desk. I think that those pages might have distracted their attention from questioning me at that point and directed my parents attention back onto the teacher because I was quickly removed from that class and I was given a new teacher, but not soon enough. There was a lot of that was done that needed to be corrected before the change.

One thing that was dealt out at me was the class clown of the school. It was a short, toothpick of a girl, with red hair, glasses, bucked-teeth, and looked like something off of the cartoon, "Dennis the Menace." She was one that always loved to kiss other boys, make fart noises with her armpits, and belch and fart as loud as she could throughout the day. She was the most disgusting girl anyone could have predicted could turn out so sweet, and she was a good friend as well at times, but I would take advantage of that at times too. She was an awesome friend outside of being a girl that any boy my age could have ever wanted.

Although she seemed happy, her gestures and emotions told people otherwise. I think that I knew her better than anyone else could have in those days, and I didn't like what I saw. I believe that was mostly because I saw myself in her eyes. Plus she would constantly wait for me in the coat closet to get my things and attempt a sneak attack to kiss me on the lips or cheeks. She planted a kiss one time on my backpack causing her to fall over and hit her head on the ground. I felt bad for her and helped her up only to have her kiss me on the lips. She then told me that I was her best friend and that she felt she could tell me anything. I found out that her father like my brother was abusing her and like my cousins were also abusing me.

I never spoke to her much after I found that out. I felt like I was totally alone in the abuse until that point. I felt ashamed to know such a secret of hers that I cried myself to sleep that night. The next day she asked me for my phone number. I gave her a long list of random numbers and then someone else came up and ruined the nasty trick I was trying to do towards her. I tried to fib my way out of it and then I ended up giving my number to her anyway. She never called me much though. Even with trying to hide the truth, I was left only to tell the truth that my parent's didn't want me to give out my phone number to strangers. I then replied, "And there's no one stranger than she is!"

At the time the geek of a girl didn't catch on to what I was saying, but she would later be a very close friend. I would find my life becoming more and more distant as the months drew by slowly. I locked myself in my room to watch, "A.L.F", play on video games, and hide from my brother for hours on end until our parents came home. My brother remained secretive in his abusive behaviors towards me as I grew up. He would chase me around the house and pull me down the stairs as I tried to run away. I would fall and he would grab my ankles and drag me back down the stairs face-first across each step. He then turned me around and tickled me until I couldn't breath, and one time I think I even saw heaven in the torture.

I don't really remember much about God being part of my life in my younger years, but I do remember my time at church with a reverend, whose name I can't remember for the life of me now. I remember Sunday school and how cold the room got, as flies would fly at the window and attempt to escape only to be blasted with the outdoors subzero cold temperatures.

I really recall when they had a play on judgment and the devil. My brother was the cutthroat judge that would put away anyone for anything and he was so strictly serious about his role that he even had my mother make him underwear that had hearts on the outside. At the end of that play the judge was to turn around and flash the audience unknowingly his underwear with the hearts on the outside of them.

I learned to never let him live that moment down. It became my way of stopping his violent behavior for the most part. I could bring up church at anytime and he would be nicer than someone giving me a million dollars everyday for a year. Not to mention he hated being embarrassed in front of his many girlfriends. Needless to say I had some leverage on his person and I could shoot some ammo at him, but the sexual and physical abuse would continue to happen. I would find myself hiding more and more from my brother and his anger issues he took out on me over the years. But the next year he was possibly the worse, and I had the grades to prove it.

Chapter 2

The Changing of the Grades!

While I was uncertain about this new found class with a new teacher that would actually pay some attention to what I was working on in class, I found a discrete way of handling my emotions through playing some video games. Oh yeah! Video games were awesome, especially when you were grounded from them. My grades from my first teacher's courses were very poor at best. It was only the first grade and I was half way through and I didn't even want to do the work any more. I was so far behind my classes that I didn't care about anything but playing during recess.

It felt like forever as my parents argued whose fault it was that I was doing so badly at my first countable year in school. One thing that was commonplace for this conversation was the fact that I was grounded. "Whatever that meant?" I thought. Little did I know that my father would explain it in further detail as a form of punishment?

"You are grounded to your room!" He yelled. "No Nintendo, no computer games, no television, no friends will come over at all!" "No friends!" I exclaimed. "Why no friends, they didn't do anything wrong why would you punish them?" All I thought about was my best friend and how he was getting food flung at him. That larger than the rest of the kids, clumsy, frail beast of a boy, and how much I would miss him and his company. Thinking to myself, "Who would help protect me from the "Rump Ranger"?"

I was immediately transferred out of that class into another class. What other forms of punishment could there be. I had no friends in this class, or so I thought. I had no one to talk with or flirt with. But one good thing about the new class was that I would be free from that devilish little redheaded girl who kept trying to make passes at my expense. I don't know why that mattered other than her grotesque nature and mannerisms for a girl out breached my own or any other boy's in that classroom.

"Wait a minute?" as I thought to myself. I would be rid of this pesky little nerdy girl, plus I would be with my giant of a friend, and I wouldn't have to listen to a stupid old hag of a teacher?" "Count me in!" I thought. "How much worse could it be with a different teacher and students?" I met with various students I had been friends with in Kindergarten. The short, well tanned, girl with pig tails, and a girl I knew from the back alley house across from my parents. Her heritage was a lot like my own. My grandfather on my mother's side was a Native American Indian. The only problem with her was that she had white skin, and she was pail with blond hair. By today's standards she looked more German than Indian. I then met back up with various other friends from my kindergarten days. The darker brown colored girl who I had a deep crush on sat next to me. She was a character all of her own. Her mannerisms were all about her. She was an Oreo-cookie, whatever that meant? She had frizzy hair that bulged out like I had never seen before. She was smart, funny, and she stood out in a lot of ways. She was my first friend of a different color that I had ever known. She was every bit as tough as the other boys in the classroom. She could run, jump, sing, and skip-to-my-lieu, she did it all in the same breath. She stood apart from all of the other athletes in the field day events, and she even took precedence over boys in many of the events. I idolized her for her talents and gifts. I wanted to be an Oreo-cookie just like her.

She was in my kindergarten class along with another boy in the new classroom. He had the smile of a bulldog and the personality of a chimpanzee. Literally! He would climb monkey bars as though they were nothing short of another way to travel the world. He flew across them as light as air could be. His face was that of a bulldog, but only because of his smile. At least that's how I saw him. He wasn't as ugly as a bulldog, but in all of his pictures his lower jaw always stuck out and his bottom teeth always showed never his top teeth. He was by far the smartest kid in the new class and he seemed to be the most collected child in the room. Then there were the two next-door neighbors of my giant friend. We called them "A" and "S". "A" and "S" were almost like cousins of sorts. S and A always seemed to be at my friends house playing outside in the yard with dirt, GI Joes, and digging tool trucks. The three of them were practically inseparable. I made the fourth of the crew of boys that would take on wrestling on the front lawn. Tag teams of S and A, along with Demon and Dragon, we wrestled each other like our favorite superstars of WWF at the time. "S" the smaller of the two friends would always show that dynamite came in small packages, as he would climb the ropes as we called them out. Not that we had turn-buckles or rope even, but in our minds we did and we set limits on hurting others because we didn't like getting hurt anymore than we liked going to see a doctor. S would climb the top rope and pound out anyone who got in his way.

Those hours, days, people, and places were what helped to keep me somewhat sociable. It was those kind of people who kept me grounded into the world around me and away from my brother's world. I still cherish those memories that God had given me to hold onto. Being away from my house and with friends meant that I wasn't getting abused and beaten by my brother. But it wasn't like we hated each other. I worshiped the ground he walked on. He seemed to have multiple girlfriends at the same time. My brother and I eventually started to get along with each other as the year progressed. Abusive sexual behavior became less that year, but it was still present. I started liking the attention. We would lie to our parents and others to keep our secret hidden so that no one would know that we were getting each other off. I hated the idea, but my brother said that no one would understand it, and I would get him into more trouble and I would be dead when he was done with me, if I told anyone about it. I was truly scared of what he would do if I didn't lie for him in any case. His rage and anger were so fierce that as I let him do things to me I felt ashamed, but more scared of being a human punching bag if I didn't let him have his way with me. I eventually found myself wanting to be away from home all of the time and away from his clutches. I ended up staying multiple nights at my grandmother's house where my cousins were living for a short while, while their stepfather was in the Navy in California. The oldest of the female cousins, of whom I was attracted to, mostly because of her long blond hair and her sexual remorse for me, was having sex with multiple people. Two of them were my other cousins, and one of the victims was her younger brother. I would find out at a later time parts of the ring-of-crimes happening were from my oldest female cousin, and my oldest boy cousin. The older male cousin would have sexual relationships with all of his cousins including my brother and I, and he would have them even with his sister at times. I too found myself having sex with his sister, which was my cousin. We all acted the part, however, we couldn't tell anyone about the things we were doing. So we made a pact to seem like normal cousins, fighting, screaming and making fun of each other in public settings. But behind closed doors in the shadows of our basement walls we all had sex together as one big pornographic, incest driven, driven crazy bunch of psychopathic kids we were at the time.

Sex was all that it seemed like our whole cousin-system had in common. That was all that we did together as kids. I remember staying out at night camping at my oldest male cousin's house. We would camp out in the backyard, wait until the adults went to sleep, then we would play truth or dare and ended up being naked running around outside of the tent just to prove that we weren't a chicken during the dare. We even would try to sneak over to my cousin's girlfriend's house to have sex with her unsuccessfully most of the time. I never had any of his girlfriends though, he was too stingy with them, or so I thought. He didn't want to get caught with me being a part of the equation. He told me I had to stay away and I could only watch them have sex. So I did the only thing I could. I walked back to the tent and waited for him to be done. I was only eight-years-old at the time, but I felt like I had been more sexed up than any prostitute that was twice my age.

I don't remember much about my second grade year at that elementary school, but I do remember having a couple girlfriends. I met a girl that liked me and even became my girlfriend only to use me to get even with another boy. I was so ashamed I pushed that boy down the stairs and I kissed the girl in front of the teachers just to prove my love for her and a point to not mess with my emotions. The other thing I remember about my second grade year was walking home with the redhead girl from the poor old woman's class of my first grade year. I propositioned her with sexual favors. I told her that I would be her boyfriend only if she would have sex with me. I can still remember the look she gave me of awe and excitement. I then remember walking away ashamed of what I had said, because I wasn't attracted to her, and I felt like I was desperate for sexual stimulation beyond my cousins' worlds. I felt like I deceived a friend's trust in me. I knew I had crushed her heart to pieces as I walked away and possibly by the proposition of how I would only be her boyfriend for sexual purposes. My world grew smaller with every blow to my ego I made. My glasses were the least of my worries that year. I think that the abuse was causing me to think even crazier thoughts than before as well. I couldn't tell my right from my left.

Chapter 3

Right or Left?

Before I go further into the story, I need to clear up a few things. Looking back at the events of my life is a hard process. I mean I still can't even remember most of what happened in my second grade year other than a girl I dated and a kid I threw down the stairs on accident. But I can tell you what happened to me that summer. In order to do this I will have to share a bit of my heritage with you.

My Grandfather was the first of the family tree born in the United States. Prior to this we were all from Ireland. They had twin babies. My grandfather and his sister, who so happened to have similar names, she would later on change her first name to a totally different one for reasons still beyond my thought processes of family hatred and obnoxious jokes. His sister didn't want a thing to do with him after a quarrel of a great magnitude broke out amongst the family after their father and mother had passed away.

She was also much nicer than the scumbag my grandfather came out of anyway. I loved my grandfather for what he was worth, but I didn't think of his worth as being very much in hindsight of what he did to me as a grandchild.

Not that he was evil or a total piece of crap, but that he had sex with his best friend's wife. Of course, my grandmother swapped with my grandfather's fling as well and so became the swapping of the wives in a medium sized family of nine children at the time. The woman my grandfather cheated his other family out of a life with became his future bride and witch to be. I might want to explain a little more about the witch part.

She was a woman, if you could call her that, in her own world full of money, power, greed, and good times coming always. She never worked a day in her life and she manipulated all of her stepchildren into performing duties of hers, as if the kids didn't seem to have enough on their plate with school and a divorce to settle into. My father said that they would be slaves to her chores and she would sit around the house all day and never lift a finger for any of them. The children did all of the cooking as she watched. But how could my grandfather rid himself of a woman such as my real grandmother? I really have no other explanation other than addiction to love and lusting after that, which is unattainable by marital standards.

It was one part lie after lie, and another part of cheating a family out of a good home. The military changes people, or so I am told. It has never done anything, but harm for my family. My father was in the military and it really screwed him up inside and out. My grandfather was even worse of a shape than my father after he was grounded due to injuries sustained in battle.

My grandfather was captured and deemed a P.O.W. in World War II, he and the few that were kept alive attempted to escape in a jeep that they stole off the enemy soldiers. In that attempt to escape they hit a land mine buried in the desert sands and the jeep blew-up, flipped over, and crushed every one of the soldiers in the jeep, including my grandfather. He sustained major injuries to his spinal column and his legs were very weak for a while, but after surgery they patched him up and sent him back out again for a second time. This time he was in France dealing with a similar foe in the same war. The all-clear call was given and he checked on several soldiers wounded in the battle, and he was shot in the back. Not just anywhere, but on the same spot where he was previously injured by the jeep. This caused him to be paralyzed from the waste down. He could walk and function, but if he hurt himself on his legs he couldn't feel it. The doctors took it very seriously and forced him to set behind a desk for the remainder of his time served. He later became involved in the department of Veteran's Affairs and started representing several soldiers who were injured in combat situations.

Who ever said you needed feeling down below the belt to have the fun in your pants come out to play for a while. My grandfather was a ladies man, and a real gentleman of sorts. He could talk to them with pristine poise and he always took them home by the end of the conversations. Several years had passed and my grandfather and grandmother were married for about ten to fifteen years before the other couple started in on their affairs. Somehow each person knew the other from previous arrangements, but they all had the same thing on their minds too. Party until the cows came home again. It seemed to be an awesome time for all of them until they found out that the other couples were with each other's significant other. Divorce was then prevalent, and so the family was torn apart by lustful thoughts of the mind.

Both men married the other man's wife, both wanted the other one's items of value, but ultimately my grandfather won the legal battle for the children. This was due to his doubled back scheming of a lifetime achievement that he so righteously earned the award for. He had the same exact lawyer as my grandmother, and neither he nor his lawyer told her that until the day of the court hearing, then she knew he had it worked out into his favor.

My grand mother left with her new man and went away for a while. They had an additional three children who didn't seem to amount to much to her husband, but then again he never amounted to anything either, according to everyone I spoke with in the present time. Two boys and a girl were born through my grandmother's second marriage. All of them were very close to one another and all of them weren't without their own problems. And yet another story could emerge further from this, but I will stick to the addiction part.

As for my grandfather and his newfound bride being in my life, it was all it was and then some. "Cue the laughter sounds in the studio!" The two of them constantly had it out for me and for my brother. My grandfather and step grandmother pitted us against one another by sending a single gift to us only labeling it one child's name and not the others. Then when my parents caught on to that trick, they started having my father's youngest sister send the gift over to whomever it was addressed to and attempt to not tell our parents about it.

That summer after my second grade year, I found my focus to be distracted in a very negative fashion. I can barely remember what happened to me, but I can remember it well enough I could still feel the ball hitting my head like a huge hunk of concrete thrown at my skull and shattering on my head. An eight ball off of the billiards table had been swung at my head knocking me down. The criminal caught in all of the commotion of the flinging was my half cousin holding an eight ball and attempting to hit me again with full force of a twelve-year-old arm. He was very interesting to say the least. I tried to not go to sleep while my mother held me tight as my step grandmother drove us to the hospital. My cousin's attempts at apologizing were very tranquil as his eyes changed from a disastrous mind to an innocent muster of kindness and shock. His apology came as one of the coldest apologies I had ever heard, even today.

As I lay in the hospital bed with a lump on my head that was the size of an 8-ball off of a billiard table, I cried and begged to get even with my cousin and punish him harshly. He did it on purpose and without even batting an eye. It was like looking at death in the face. His whole reasoning behind the act of bashing me over the head with the ball was that he wanted to see what would happen.

The following weekend I was asked to stay the night again. This time my psychotic cousin wouldn't be there to bash me over the head again. I was scared of the dark, of my cousins, of my brother, and of the idea of my life being taken while I was asleep at a place I didn't trust with my life. I stayed up most of the night eyes opened and people handling me with their tired and aggressively touching my body as I attempted to fall asleep. I left the room crying and asking to go home. I was scared and alone in that house. Our step grandmother got out of bed with very little effort and grabbed me by the arm and pulled me with her by the phone and called my parents. My brother was angry with me, but I didn't care. I didn't want to feel this way ever again. She contacted my parents and told them to pick me and my brother up and that we were never to come out there again to stay the night. She called me a crybaby and insulted me along with the other cousins because I kept them all up.

My parents heard the story about what had happened and what my dad's stepmother said to me. My father reprimanded her for being so cruel towards me when I was so scared. Then he told her that his children were never coming back out to her house even if they chose to on their own.

What had caused me even more damage and became a problem for me was that my brother and cousins were having their fun watching the "Naked Women Channel." They talked about teenaged things like sex and masturbation. They talked about what they were going to do to me when the lights went out. I think I had a reason to cry that night, but I wasn't about to snitch on my brother or my cousins because the punishment for that would have been much worse than telling a lie.

That summer I joined a bowling league for children. With sports as an afterthought, due to my run-ins with crooked baseball coaches, swindling Cub Scout troops and an eight ball hitting me in the back of my head, I felt I was going to hate playing that sport as well. It turned out that I was good, really good at bowling. This was a way for me to get much of my aggression out of my system from the stresses of life, and living with my brother and cousins.

I had control of my own destiny for once and I was bowling against professional bowlers and winning against them. My courage grew and I was doing my best to stay clear of anything other than bowling. People looked at me in a different light, and I was in control for once. And I would imagine my family and enemies as the pins and I would release my anger at them most of the time getting strikes and forcing other bowlers to bow out of tournaments due to my approaching professional status, as I seemed to win at everything that year. Bowling made me feel alive for the first time, but I knew it wouldn't last forever.

The summer had to end soon and I needed to go back to school. I tried so hard to forget about the abuse and sex that was forced upon me that summer. I kept imagining that I was a superstar in bowling, and that I could out whit the best of the best bowlers. My imagination started running wild as time progressed and as I lost sleep at night staying awake to fend myself from my brother's torture.

I was free when I was in my bowling lane. I was perfection at its finest hour. I had to return to school for another year of hell. My teacher was a skinny, dark-haired woman, with a mole on her nose that made her look like a witch, but she had a smile that melted fear away. This was my third grade class year. This was where I could possibly change my whole life. This was where I forgot a lot of things about my past and I forgot about my brother's mean outlook on my life. This was also where I forgot how to write! I couldn't remember if I was right-handed or left-handed. I found out I could draw waves and not just straight lines. I seemed to write the same with both hands, but ultimately I was predominately right-handed.

Even though my ego was gone to waste in school and at home I daydreamed even more and I asked our teacher the dumbest question I could have asked, "Am I right-handed or left-handed?" Of course she couldn't tell me. I had to find out for myself. Both sides were uncomfortable, and both were a bit out of sorts to me. I think that the crack to the head from my cousin's eight ball caused more damage than I had thought originally.

To see the look on my teachers face after asking her the question, it was a puzzled look like she couldn't help me with it. The rest of the children were too busy laughing at the question and making fun of me in my new glasses, and to add the fact that I asked the teacher if I was right handed or left handed was an added bonus to my humiliation. I was doomed from the start of the school year, and the fact that I was the shortest kid in the classroom didn't even seem so bad as compared to the rest of the comments made about how stupid I was. But being short also had some advantages, I could sleep in the back of the class without getting seen, and I didn't have to duck going through the steam tunnel hallway.

Back at home I would continue my punishment on a daily basis as my brother continued to pin me to the ground, tickle me until I was blue in the face, and then force his penis into my mouth while I was opened up crying. I had a much harder time sleeping than what most people thought. If it wasn't a lack of sleep for me it was the issue of wetting my bed because I was too tired to get up. I was nine-years-old and still wetting the bed. My parents tried to find out why I was always wetting my bed. I could have told them it was because my brother scares me and makes it so I couldn't sleep. But their answer worked as well. They said that I was just lazy and needed to wake up and go in the middle of the night. When as it turned out I would wake up in my dreams, but not in reality and use my dream's restroom. It felt good and kept me warm throughout the night, as the winter months would come around. My bruising and scaring were on the inside of my body. Places where people couldn't see the problems occurring.

God seemed to not care whether I lived or died. I didn't really know why I thought that way, but I could tell my life was already bad in comparison to other people's lives. And yet other children in my class would make fun of my appearance due to my parent's lack of style in clothing. I didn't really care though; I was warm with my long-underwear on and snow boots with big bird sown on the side. I seemed to get into verbal fights with kids on a daily basis, but I never showed up for the actual fight. I usually left the school a different route.

One night our family came home to a broken in door and window. Messy people had robbed our house. They turned over beds, threw around our clothes, attempted to pick gun locks off of my father's rifles, and they left a blood trail where they cut themselves with glass that they smashed to get inside of our house. I did feel a bit scared, but I did enjoy the fact that my brother was just as scared and violated that night as I was and he would end up not sleeping very well for one night. I slept very sound and without my brother there to bother me. Revenge of a Godly wrath is very bitter and yet very sweet on my watch. I can't think of a better way to scare my brother than to violate his things and get away with it. But that same night they stole our VCR, which was recording the "A-Team!" "Awe, even God has a sense of humor and is laughing at me!" But we got the last laugh on the crooks. We had a wired remote that they left behind and that remote was the only thing that would control the VCR for just about all of it's' functionality. I guess they didn't get to watch the A-Team either.

Chapter 4

Nothing but a Dead End!

One of the hardest things for me to learn about myself was that I had limits to everything I did. Those limits scared me when I broke them. My brother, my cousins, and my friends all seemed needed of my services at some point in my life. I stretched out my arms and held them when they needed it. I cared for those who showed me compassion as I saw it. I listened to those whose problems seemed worse than my own at the time. At age 10 I was a leading child psychologist. Not literally, but I felt like I was one, and from that day on I felt like a pin cushion waiting for the poke of another person waiting to take a chunk of hide out of me. I had enough of it, as I was very fat and lazy according to my brother and my parents.

Before I go too much further into this part of my story, however, I would like to say that my life wasn't always being abused. I was not always a victim of sex and lies. I had a normal life outside of this formal behavior. Many of the cuts and bruises around my body were self-inflicting from clumsy stumbles to riding my youngest cousin's bike into a dead-end sign. Yeah! That really hurt a bunch. But had I not done that then I wouldn't have gotten to see the "Blue Angels air show" fly over my head. God sent me angels to intercede.

I didn't ask for God's help with the situations, but it did cheer me up as I was carried into my hippy of an aunt's house. She was literally a hippy stylish dressed woman and she was tall.

To describe this aunt of mine would be like describing a stereotypical hippy. She had long dirty-blond hair, round coke-bottle glasses, and an attitude that only a chemical could produce. Her boyfriend was the same style only he had curly, bushy white hair that showed streaks of where he was darker colored at some point in his lifetime.

My aunt was the type of person who would never stop kissing other people's butts for the benefit of self-loathing, and gaining brownie points with her father, my dad's father as well, and my grandfather's newer modeled wife. If the stepmother was around you could almost be sure that my aunt was close behind. As I crashed the little girls bike with pink trimmings and the pompom handles, I saw myself wanting to be held by my mother. Instead I got the blue angels in the sky, and the two cousins who raped me carrying me into the house making sure I didn't pass out. Some good that did, I started sleeping right away in the reclining chair and awoke when my parents showed up with their car to take me to the hospital to get stitched up from being cut by the sign and barbwire fence that lay on the ground where I stopped.

My life was a whole series of bumps and bruises. Most of those bruises and cuts were made from my stupid mistakes. If you added to that the choices that I made with my brother's fists cocked and loaded for my head, I did what any child of 10 years old would do in that situation, "Cry!"

My choices were few and far in between good and bad. It was survive or die as my decisions with an older brother who had already threw me down stairs, punched me, kicked me, scratched me, bit me, and sexually assaulted me at night. I was his personal real-life punching bag for years. Along with that I was his sex toy that couldn't do much to defend myself against a boy twice my size and age. That summer it could have all ended for him and for me. I didn't have the gull to get him into trouble at the time though.

My brother always seemed to have a problem with keeping girlfriends, partly due to my Casanova way's of smooth talking to them, or my parents constantly grounding my brother I forget which one of the two really worked. But he had a girlfriend that was a beautiful young and attractive girl that was a year or two younger than he was.

Everyone called her a moose. I don't know why but I think it had to do with something she put into her hair. She was with him everywhere my brother went. They were inseparable and attached at the lips except for the one time she was playing truth or dare in the back of a tour bus that they had been on for a band trip.

The band members invited me back gathered around and she asked if I have ever been "French Kissed by a girl before?" I replied, "Sure hasn't every guy?" She then asked me to kiss her with a "French Kiss," then she asked how I learned how to kiss so well. I told her my brother showed me. Staring back at his direction, I could see the anger in his eyes flaring up with fire and sparks of lightening directed at my head. "I meant I saw him do it with his ex-girlfriends! Its not like it's hard or anything!" I continued with a smirk and a saving grace of a smile and a sigh of relief.

To further the blow to my brother's manhood, she said that I kissed way better than my brother! That remark from her almost put me into intensive care at the hospital. I had never seen my brother get so angry at her or at me. He called me things I didn't even know existed until he spat them out of his mouth with flairs of fire from the pit of hell that was engulfing his heart.

I kind of wished I had stuck with my first instincts and said, "Yeah! My brother taught me how to do it!" "He kisses on me all the time and my penis as well!" That would have shown him, but I was afraid of the outcome in either situation so I stuck with the less violent of the two results.

We finally made our trip to the band camp and unloaded our instruments. We all slept in barracks in an old military base that was used that year for marching and drills for band marches. The barracks were dirty with cobwebs and various other critters of insects crawling around at night. I decided to go to sleep earlier than the other people because I was afraid of what might happen to a little guy like me in the night.

My brother and a few band members attempted to pull pranks on me throughout the night. One band-geek tried to make me wet the bed by putting my hand into a bowl of warm water. I rolled over and kicked him in his family jewels. He dropped the water and his body went limp for about an hour.

Another sucker, I mean band member attempted to put shaving cream in my hand and force me to itch my face. I didn't fall for that trick. After all I had an older brother that I dealt with for years before I met up with these brainless wimps. Plus my brother was not really around parse that he could tell them my secrets. One thing my brother didn't count on in those day's was my ability to roll around on the bed and hit people with precise shots to the groin area, and all while I was asleep.

The worst thing that I got was a sock on my head and toothpaste stuck on my shorts. They didn't dare get too close to me. I was a loose canon in my sleep. It was almost like I was sleep walking or God was controlling my actions to keep me safe from their stupid pranks.

Every year about the same time the school had a celebration of Las Vegas. Showgirls, jazz music, tuxedos and women in shiny dresses all around my brother, but that year would be different than years past. That year they needed a new stage and a design behind it. My brother used all his artistic talents to help design a stage.

He took an old child's record player design and made a terrific backdrop. It was a drum with a drum major's staff. The character had red and black clothing, which matched the school colors perfectly, and they had the backdrop for the new Las Vegas Show of that year. I don't recall getting much more abuse after that day from my brother.

We did act like brothers on a normal level as well. We kicked, bit, fought, and threw each other around the room, hit each other in the groin, or just throw a ball at the other person's head. That part was brotherly love, and the name-calling was a standard feature that came with the package as well.

Our mother was very lenient on us boys for most of our days, but if we said any swear words it was with a bar of soap for either of us. We didn't like to use those words too often. Ivory soap tastes very bad when you just don't know what you said wrong the first few bites.

But that summer I felt more invincible than I had felt before. Something came over me in my pride took me for a ride in the limousine to show me off. That summer my cousins and I all played tackle football, and various other games like smear-the-queer. Not a very good title for a game, but I guess it worked with my brother and cousins.

For some reason in those games I always got the ball. Then I would get tackled. After getting tackled, I swear someone touched my snicker's candy bar I had in my pocket. My snicker was fondled. Ewe!

Even though I was feeling more and more invincible, I was still more afraid of what my brother could do to me. I carried three larger than me, boys down a one hundred yard patch of land where we played football, but I was still very terrified of my brother.

At the end of that summer, my two half-cousin's moved away with their stepfather and real mother to California for two years. I was done with being sexually run through for a little while.

That time would prove to be a huge relief of sexual abuse from all of my family, but this also is where my addictive sexual behaviors started to show their true colors. It was that summer that I really drew closer to my giant of a friend that I had met in our first grade lunchroom extravaganza. The big oaf and his techniques for wrestling were amazing at best. I wasn't about to wrestle a two hundred pound five-foot, nine-inch tall boy that was already balding from wearing too many hats and genetic makeup of his father's side of the family. The poor kid didn't have a chance. He did have a girlfriend though, which is more than I could have ever said for myself.

He seemed to get all of the girls that I wanted that summer. I did end up almost sleeping with his neighbor twins and made it almost all the way until that silly boy giant stepped in and cock-blocked my game at age 11. Can you believe that? This started my curse of having no sex after having been sexual since I was five years old.

Truthfully sex became my way to show love and affection. Every girl that liked me or I liked I wanted to have sex with. It was the only way I knew if someone loved me. I was still feeling very alone with my cousins gone, about the issue of not having sex, which I started to masturbate a little at night.

I would isolate myself in my room as my brother went off to school, then the military. I began to find my father's stash of pornographic pictures, magazines, and videos. My father had a huge drawer full of pornographic material and I was all for it. I don't believe I ever got caught. I stored most of the one's I liked under my bed or in a drawer so that no one else knew I had them. I ended up in a lot of trouble at the beginning of my fourth grade year.

I remember I missed a lot of class that year due to a technique that I found out I could do. I called it sneezing on command. I had everyone fooled for a while. I was missing day after day of school just to catch up on sleep and play videogames while I was pretty much alone at home. My grandmother on my mother's side of the family watched me then. So yeah I was alone.

Without the sex in my life, my mind wondered freely about everyday. My imagination constantly got me into trouble. I stole candy from store counters as clerks saw what I had taken. I didn't even know I had taken the candy. One time I beat up a loaf of bread as I talked to it like it was my big brother back from the Army.

I snuck around the school hallways many times just to imagine myself being a spy going to the bathroom. One day I was caught by a heavy set teacher who loved me to death, but felt I was up to no good and sent me back to class where I peed my pants in front of the class.

Beyond that I felt like a normal child in the fourth grade. I would daydream my time away in school except for in music class. That was one subject matter I loved to be in. Reading, writing, and arithmetic were my least favorite subjects in school followed by science.

That year in my elementary school, either the kids loved me or hated me. There seemed to be no middle ground for affection or hatred towards my character. My only goals I set out to achieve that year were to be nice to the teachers, perverted towards the girls, and rude to the athletic boys. The next thing I remembered from all of that action was that summer was coming around the corner.

I graced my presence around my posy of women at the local public pools. All of them greeted me with a smile or a smirk. I knew I was a cool person with my hot-fired boxer style swim trunks. The lifeguard saved me a time or two as well. Helped me to fake the drowning, but I was cautious about every move I made. I would cop a feel of the ladies as they walked by.

Thank the lord for public swimming pools. Not really! These were places that actually made my addiction worse. What I was retaining in school over the previous years was becoming lost to sleep deprivation and sexual fantasies of other children in my class. I still wonder if that eight ball did more damage than what I thought. My life at that point on would cause me to go into more lying and cheating others out of their lives.

Chapter 5

Highest of the lowest rung

In the fifth grade at my elementary school, it was an honor to be a crossing guard. I don't recall the reason why I wanted to be one other than the trip to the amusement park after the school year was out. I got to tell other kids what to do and when to do it. That was about the fun of that moment.

While most of the students were trained in the fourth grade year to become crossing guards, I was added to the roster in the fifth grade. I wanted to be trained by our fifth grade instructor Mr. T. He wasn't the A-Team's golden-rings and other things type of person, but he was a person whom I looked up to. He was also my brother's fifth grade teacher, which made me all the more nervous.

My problems with all of these issues with my brother were where finding out where they all started. Thinking back on them one thing that all of my cousins had in common were the teacher Mr. T.

My fourth grade teacher, the hall monitoring, loving hippo of a woman, with an even bigger heart, always looked out for my best interests. She was like a second mother while I was in school. I always seemed to have healing parents even when my real one's weren't there all the time.

This teacher was nice beyond measure, yet she had a stern outlook on life. I found out later that I resembled her son's image to almost a perfect match. The reason I bring both teachers up was that they were mostly in cooperation, but to me they were competing for teacher of the year. They both had the talent to become a school principal in the future. But neither one of them would care to step on the other one's toes.

He was one of the greatest people I had ever been able to look up to as a person. He had a talent with children that I adored and looked out for. He could be strict with the children if he wanted to, but he would much rather be gentle with the kids and less of a disciplinarian. He had the heart of a true leader, and yet the school board would pass him by for a principal position every year he tried.

Eventually he was diagnosed with cancer the last time I heard of him from another teacher, but I hadn't heard anything else about his scholastic days since. He would allow his students to grade other student's work, but that was really just to test their knowledge of the subject matter.

I never got to grade any of the work, but that was all right with me. He made me feel accepted by the world even though other children in the class wouldn't even acknowledge my existence. He made my nerdy-ness seem out of place for those who teased me for my glasses and intellect. Having glasses in those days meant you were a four eyed freak and a loser of a wimp. I chased girls around the playground that called me names. I even kissed a few of them to spread the infectious cootie bug around the girls. I made it to first base with at least four of the girls that year. But to hear them describe the experience it wasn't all it was cracked up to be.

I was an eleven-year-old boy who always had an excuse for every situation I was in. I walked the halls of my elementary school like I had something to show the world up my nose. My head was held up high with pride for a while until the talent show. Then I was tormented into thinking I would have been better off staying home for that experience. That was because it was when the group "New Kids" was popular and together for the first round of celebrity stardom. I was king of my own world until that day.

My face turned a beat red as I did a skit with my nerdy girl friend with the red hair, and my new girlfriend who I really liked a lot. She was a dark haired; blue eyed, glasses included, and she was a hot woman of a freak. She would make me feel so welcomed in everything we did that I had a crush on her just to be with her on a daily basis. But I was lacking talent at the talent show that year, and I tripped over myself during the performance of a couple songs sung by the aforementioned group. We sounded as bad as we looked, but we made it through the end and it ended up not being so bad after all. The other kids clapped and booed us off the stage and then it was on to the next talented show.

I tend to think that my older brother held a record for the world's worst troublemaker in the school until I came along. I did manage to allow him time to keep his record for about a week. Then I took his dirty joke book to school and started to tell others jokes right from the pages only to have it taken away from me in the first hour of having fun with it. Mr. T was not amused by any of it.

Later that day I found it in the office where the school secretary was busy typing and staring me down as if she knew what was already about to happen to me before I did. I felt like a punch line out of the book of dirty jokes. Although it didn't seem that funny to me at the time, I can look back and laugh at it now.

My parents being eager to ground me for a week at a time would hide the power supply and RF adapter of my gaming systems so that I couldn't play them. But I quickly sniffed them out and strolled past my grandmother who was watching soap operas rather than me, and I had my video games back in my clutches.

One thing that I learned as an addict is that if we have an addiction to something we will go to any length to get it and risk further persecution to obtain it if necessary. I was definitely no exception to that rule. In fact, lying was the one thing that I was better at than video games. By this time in my life, lying was a part of my daily routine. If I didn't lie, I couldn't breath on my own. I was so good at avoiding the truth that I wasn't even sure if I was telling the truth or lying about telling a lie. I was a compulsive talker and liar that year. It mostly had to do with the fact that if I told people the truths that it would sound more like a lie than the lie I told did.

That summer helped me further my addictive behavior beyond anything else in my life. This would be the turning point into more of an addiction than anything else. My giant of a friend and another youthful friend were constantly competing for my attention. The days would go back and forth between the two. One day would be with the Giant kid, the next it would be with the scrawny kid down the street.

I enjoyed the giant more than the scrawny most of the time. He had neighbors that were hot little twin girls about my age, and they were in love with me. My giant of a friend would end up dating the twins' older sister, and one of the twins ended up sleeping with the scrawny kid down the street. I still don't know how that happened. My giant friend and I were closer to each other that year more so than previously explained. My giant friend's family made me feels at home. That is with one exception, he had a kid sister who I didn't feel like having around much. That was mostly because I thought she was ugly and very uncoordinated at her age. Plus she was a giant as well for her age. A part of me felt sorry for her, and the other part told me to stay away. For the longest time I listened to that part, but it wasn't long before she grasped my many body parts and attempted to have her childhood ways with me. I just don't know how many times I passed on her throwing herself at me, but it was a lot.

She loved her brother to bring over friends as she clung to their every move. I kicked her off my legs a time or two. She was a virus that wouldn't go away, a knot you couldn't untie until you cut the strings, and she was so darned cute for a little girl that you hated the attention the way she was giving it that you hated even more to push her away because it would make her cry and feel rejected.

My feelings for her were always like a brother's feelings towards a sister, strictly platonic and nothing more, but she always skipped the sisterly love and went for the more factors. She was so desperate that summer that she worked out a play to trap me in a basement staircase with her and her giant brother on top of the doorway out of that cage. She had managed an all out plan of attach on my will for loving her as only a sister. She set me up for a date with one of her twin friends next door, and then she would trap her and her "man-meat" (Me!) in a that cage causing me to panic. They were using pirate games to trap us in the dungeon, and my giant of a friend decided that he was going to put his sister in there with me. Life is cruel, as you will soon read.

While his sister and I were in this dungeon, he thought it would be even more fun to sit on the top of the doors making it nearly impossible to get out.

As tension rose in the chamber below that giant of a friend, his sister was fondling her man-meat. I on the other hand was pounding at the door and at the chance to break free from her clutches. She began to talk about weddings and how we were meant to be together and how she loved me, and then at that moment I ran down the stairs into the corner pushed his sister out of my way and leaped at the doorway.

I must have pushed really hard, because when I looked back I was up off of the ground, my giant friend was flying one direction and one of the twins next door was flying in the other direction with my friend's sister's head poking out of the dungeon steps. Her words were perfect in timing. "Sorry…" she said with a squeaky little mouse voice. Her words sent me into a quick leap of faith at the doors. His sister told me that I never even touched the steps. I just flew out of the stairwell and landed. It seemed as though God had picked me up and carried me out of that situation. It was an amazing feat of strength from outside of my own doing. It would have been an even better summer than last year except for one thing.

My cousin's decided to come back into my life. They came back from California, and my older girl cousin and my other younger hippy cousin were sexing me up again, but one good thing did come out of that summer that was awesome. My brother left for the military.

There he broke his leg while marching with full gear while working on drills with his platoon. He went through the entire basic training with a cast on his leg and made his frustrations well known to the whole group of soldiers. His training was said by him to be the hardest thing he had ever done before.

But the summer started getting even better when I was hitting it off with one of the twins next to my giant friend. The hotter sister of course, and she wanted me as much as I wanted her. In fact we attempted to have a bunch of sex with each other in my giant friend's sister's room, until my giant of a friend steamrolled his way into the room and blocked the plays I was making on a twin girl with a possible three-way tie. To my sickening mind it was a sad and desperate moment that God himself caused me to break out into tears of madness and anger for my giant of a friend. I did forgive him for walking in, but it was still something that I was afraid of doing again. He walked in like a ninja ready to pounce. No one heard him coming. That was just crazy. He was a giant. I dropped a 1 on that dice roll.

As I began writing about my story and my experience with sexual addiction, I have realized even now how much more this illness, this disease, and this addiction can ruin a person's life without any thought for others lives being ruined as well.

I still believe that God did stop that plan of mine from happening that day, but he had a much greater plan for me in the future. God seemed to constantly be on the look out for my well-being at specific times in my life. I was never arrested for any crimes; I never actually had sexual relations with women other than the occasional cousin or two. It was as though when people would try to be with me something would come over their minds and break through their eyes and forcibly say no I can't do this. No to you! It was like God had stepped in to wake me out of a fantasy world that I created and made me move back into the abusive situations that I had no control over. God showed me more suffering, or was that I showed myself more suffering. I believe it was a bit of both.

Chapter 6

New Kids in a School Block

A new year had arrived. I was not about to let anything or anyone push me around. Especially after I was knocked around all through elementary school. I really felt invincible again for about the first five minutes with my giant of a friend, as we stood at the entrance to our middle school.

The teachers were all in the stairway going into the building and we were told several rules to follow our first day. We were assigned lockers, a homeroom, and a teacher for the tour of the school. But I think it was possibly the first day from hell.

The teachers would have all of the students practice opening their lockers, over and over again. A vice-principal told us that we needed to be as fast as Bart Simpson on the Simpson's. It didn't matter that we were new kids in a new and scary environment where puberty was blooming in the older children and the younger ones were still speaking like little girls. Add to that mix the feeling of being lost in a huge school where every time a bell rang out we were switching to a new room and a new teacher.

Every period the bell would tell us when to go and when we needed to be in our seats. It was like being in prison only with better-looking guards and even better looking cellmates. But the food was bad all the time, and the people were constantly fighting. There were seventh and eighth grade girls that were pregnant even. The whole image was hard to fathom at first glance. You always had to look twice to make sure of what you saw. There was one boy beating another one senseless in the bathroom, a girl beating up a boy for touching her breasts and attempting to molest her in the girls' bathroom.

The bullies would be sweeping the school hallways for lost souls to pick on and beat for lunch money. I of course was smart about it. I stayed out of the halls while the bells were ringing and waited until it was about time for class to start. Either that or not bring money and bring a bagged lunch, but usually that meant not eating at all, or putting dollar bills in your shoes. They didn't seem to search the shoes due to the risk of smelling nasty feet.

Once we were past all of the flames and famine, we made our way to the various classes including my favorite class, "Music."

Why was it my favorite class? Because it had the prettiest woman as a vocal teacher, and she had a beautiful voice to match, not that I wanted to sleep with her or anything, but just that she was a soprano vocalist and she carried her voice very well. She had an opera sound to her words and you could hear her all the way to the back of the auditorium without sound equipment.

Choir became my art. I sang for many people at a time. I loved it and enjoyed the applause of the crowds that would come crashing around. People would ask me if I practiced a lot or if it was just talent. I lied and said a bit of both. Actually I practiced daily, but God had given me a beautiful voice for a male singer. I was told that I sing like nothing else heard on stage in a long while. Whatever that meant. Actually I was very good. So good in fact that I was in almost every song as the soloist.

Plus I found chorus class to be a more rewarding class than Physical Education or Art class. The singing was my form of art and physical education.

I found that singing came more naturally me than playing an instrument like my brother played. I started out playing the trumpet, but grew tired of it because my brother was always better than me at it. So I went to the piano instead. Don't get me wrong, I loved playing the trumpet as much because of the music, but when I was still in grade school I had my very first and only recital and right before playing I sprayed myself with gasoline while trying to save my parents the money of going past ten dollars at the pump. The gas trigger was stuck as I went to pull it out of the car and the gas sprayed almost every inch of my body.

I smelled of gas and gas fumes evaporated around me. I was so scared that if the room were to get too hot that I would spontaneously combust and burn up the room. And after that recital I never went to play my trumpet again. So I picked up a little bit of piano lessons, but even then I wasn't great. It was mostly because I couldn't read music very well. Any form of second language came very hard for me to learn. Something in my brain was set up wrong for learning a new language of any type. So I stuck with the American English language and a bit of sign language for my uncle who is deaf from birth defects. That made it hard to invite him to come to my concerts in school. But I managed it without him listening.

Heading back to the sixth grade year, I found more and more bullies throughout my school year. I found more trouble that year than any other school year in my history of school days. I found they were much more diverse in size and muscular tone. All of them were bigger than me!

That was the first year I met the "Dumb" brothers. The reason I called them that is for their resemblance to the Alice and Wonderland characters with their stripped shirts and ball caps with propellers on the top. Yep they were the dumb brother twins. Of course one was older than the other by a year or two, but everyone thought that they were twins because they were in the same grade.

The Dumb brothers were obnoxious, rude, and I don't even think that they took baths at all. They had brown specks on their teeth and they always had dirt in their hair. I don't recall a day where one of the two wasn't in a fight with someone. But these two bullies of children were different than the bullies I faced in elementary school.

My bully was a scrawny little nothing kid that just wouldn't leave me alone. I think he was trying to impress a girl until I threw him down the stairs as he tried to punch me in the stomach. I also used him as a punching bag with the help of another student that I fell out of touch with later. He held that bully so that I could be rid of him for good. After all I already had one bully of a brother to deal with. Not to mention my cousins.

The bully and I became friends after that day, but then we started doing crazy things a couple times on our way home from school. He showed me how fun it was to throw rocks at windows of houses and how cool it was to watch them shatter. Just then a man came running out of the house and started chasing after us. Lucky for us both the man ran out of breath and didn't see where we went.

We gave the man the slip for a little while longer, and then I walked home. I felt like I was being watched from every angle, and even though it felt good to break those windows, I felt bad that the man was so angry with us for it. It felt good to be a bad kid for once in my life though and not get caught. I eventually took my same aggressions out on by stuffed animals. Most of my anger was with my brother for not allowing me to sleep at night all of those years, and for hurting me in the butt.

Going back to the "Dumb" brothers, I in a similar situation with them, times two. The words that they spoke would make a sailor blush at times, and their attitude towards people in general made for a bad day. I remember thinking to my self; I wonder if my brother's old baby sitter would approve of their tactics. They would probably have gotten the bar and the liquid soap.

Now knowing what I knew about what the church was as a child was that only good people went there and cursing the lord was not something children of God would do. So to see those two young men digging holes in the Church garden and with the pastor at that, they must have been in trouble or something, but then I saw several kids from school around the corner and more adults helping plant trees and flowers. I could feel the lightening that God sent through me to jumpstart my heart as I about stopped breathing for a minute.

The minute the pastor came over to me and asked if I would like to come help, I didn't know what to say. I did ask him if he knew who those two boys were, and he said, "Why Yes! I do know them!" "They have been coming for weeks now!" I thought to myself they really need it. Then something came over me like a flash, and I was thinking to myself if they need it maybe I do too?

That pastor then asked me for my phone number and he would be in touch. He already knew my parents, and he wanted me there to help bring them into God's house. He then told me something that I had never heard from any one before. He told me that God loved me. God loves these two hooligans as well.

Then I found the pastor was walking around the church introducing me to the other youth. Most of them I knew from school. But some came from as far as 30 miles just to come and be with God's own children. There I found my heart melting at the chance to do what I was so long ago asked to do. So I started going to church again.

My sexual urges didn't even begin to bother me while I was in the presence of a God that loved me. But the problems started when I realized to some degree that I didn't know what love was for me. I had a feeling like I had never experienced love before, at least not without the sexual parts. I had never felt real love. I knew attraction, and I knew of caring for another person, but I hadn't been loved before. Just when I gathered my self back to the thought of love, I glanced and saw all of the girls that were in the group. I thought to myself, "Now there's love in them women!"

My addictive thinking would burst out like a welding sword of a knight standing at attention. "And these are the girls of the group!" the pastor explained. I was thinking to myself, I know most of them and I really want to know them better. But I didn't know how out of place I felt until I got a cold shoulder from all of the girls at first. All of them were around my age either a year younger or a year older. Age didn't matter to me, but I was more worried that I would say something dumb and spill my beans about how I love having sex. So I did the next best thing. I hugged them, and I tried to gain their affections, to no avail I was unsuccessful in all attempts.

While I felt a comforting presence going there it wasn't the same without that pastor to help guide me through the ruckus of people that went there. I felt distant from the rest of them almost as though I stuck out like a sore thumb. It was even harder to keep my mind set on God's love and God's will for me.

Those girls constantly rejected me multiple times. I would get passed up by them all in the halls of the school, and I never received more than a "hello" or a "hi". Where was the love, the sex, the passion, and why was I thinking that this was love.

I would listen to the girls speak about other boys in the group. "That one is hot" "Well, that one is on fire" and "you know you are not even going to go there with him like that?" Most of the bad stuff was directed towards me on a regular basis. Rejection seemed to be a form of attention at some point. People were cruel so many times when the pastor wasn't around. I guess that was why I needed him there.

I discovered masturbation that year as well. Preoccupied with my own intentions and never leaving a girl out of my imagination, I started dreaming of them all in my sleep and in the daytime I would think of them at school. I would bump into them in the hallway literally to cop a feel of youth girl booty. To most people this would seem sick and demeaning, but to me it was as close to a girl as I had gotten since my cousins sexed me up and down. Plus I felt that it was the way to get a girl to like you, not thinking it was really creeping them out of their minds.

Seeing the things that went on in the church made me even more uncomfortable about my own sexuality. That education made my situation feel that much worse as we talked about perpetrators and sex offenders in some of the youth group classes. I felt like squirming into a corner where the roaches lived I would fit in with them just fine. That's about all I thought about myself for weeks. Not about God's love over me, but the sinful nature that my acts were spreading towards those who were innocent in their own ways. And adding in the idea that not having sex before marriage made me all the more want to get married because I felt like I had done something even more morally wrong. I didn't think about it all not being my fault. So I felt the shamefulness of the acts that were pushed into my life so young.

I felt like I was born a bad person, and so I kept the secrets of my earlier days a secret from everyone including myself. I didn't want to be known as the child who had sex with my family. It was bad enough that I had the compulsivity to touch girls' private parts while walking away from them or around them.

Being accepted was hard for most boys my age, but adding in the abuse a sexual thinking at such a young age causes even deeper relationship issues. These issues force a person to either run away from the problem like I did, or to tuck it in and wait until the right day to crack and blast the hallways of a school with flailing bullets. I know now because back then I had thought about it.

I tucked my anger away from the world and took it all out each night on stuffed animals and a mat that I got to help me lose weight. Neither got rid of the anger, but they did allow me to get tired and focus away from those people whom I cared for at school.

I became a student that was the class clown style and I poked fun at everyone's expense. It gave me a bruised ego, a black eye, and a lot of shame to the boy who gave it to me in place of my guilt.

That summer due to that fight I started learning about Tae Kwon Do, and how to shut my mouth before I got into too much more trouble. Have you ever been to a work camp with a van full of hot young women? Me either, they were all nagging. That summer along with Tae Kwon Do I went to work camp.

It was a place where youth leaders didn't know where you were at night and it felt and seemed just like those times again with my cousins in their back yard going out naked and doing stupid things to attract attention to your genitals, either that or have sex in the woods. Neither of which happened to me, but several others had it done with them from all of the commotion shown around the camp the next morning. Yep, I slept right through the action.

Chapter 7

How big is yours?

Have you ever helped build a log cabin? Have you ever got a person so mad at you that they took your jacket and threw it into the boy's toilet, and then blamed everyone else after feeling guilty? Have you ever mad another person mad for calling their girlfriend a whore for not wanting to date you over them?

I have had to deal with a lot of my own doing of things. I had words that would wound people to the core. I became my own sailor. The idea that I could call a girl in the 6th grade a slut or a whore is beyond my comprehension today, but I did it and I got a blasted up face for it.

The boy who's girlfriend I insulted wasn't much to look at, or so I thought. We were friends then, but I hated how she took him away from everyone's attention including my own at times. He was popular to most of us and he was gentle to the touch, but if you got him mad and were on the other end of a fist fight be sure that he didn't hit you otherwise something would be breaking for certain. I know I was the other end of his fist.

This young man was very cool to be around, but if you were on his bad side he took things personal. He wasn't much of a fighter unless you made him want to fight you. His dark hair, blue eyes, and fists as hard as rocks made him a pretty boy almost like Charlie Sheen.

Sex addiction and love addiction will make a person do stupid things throughout their life if not treated correctly. I was no exception to that rule. I opened my mouth and everything that came out was vulgar at best. I had the worst intentions because I found myself wanting a girl that I couldn't have, and I hated how she would flaunt her stuff around the school. It caused me to have erection and embarrassed my personal spaces.

It felt as though something was putting the hurt on me for going to church for the first time continuously. The boy, who looked like Charlie Sheen, began his punching fest with my face and I went down a couple of times and he was gentleman-like in all of his actions. I was truly in the wrong, but I didn't want to be.

There were many reasons for this being the worst year of school in my whole history. First was that I wasn't out of school yet, and second I hadn't had sexual relations in over a years time. I did get some wood that summer, at summer camp with my church. Yep I helped to build a log cabin.

The first question you should always ask about building a log cabin for me was, "Why are we building a log cabin clear out here for no reason?" Well there was a reason for it. It was for a pastor and his family to live several years of their lives in total tranquility and without electronics or other amenities. They hunted for their food, farmed the limited land that they had, and built their home with a little help from our work camp group that year. It was a sticky situation all around with all of that sap on the logs. The one thing I got out of that experience was that I smelled piney-fresh after peeling the logs. The sent would stay on the workers that did that job for the day for the rest of the week. And if the smell wasn't bad enough, the sticky sap on the logs was enough to make you lose clothes as you slid down the log peeling the bark back with an old potato peeling type of device for trees.

My clothes wouldn't survive a day of this type of work. Stripping down a log takes a whole day per log. No one would expect to have found the log so hard except to see the pastor that was building the cabin work the logs it was almost an effortless task for his strong body. One other good thing about building a log cabin and getting sap all over your hands is that it makes it so you don't want to masturbate for a while.

In all of the exciting things we did at the work camp, I think that my favorite thing to do was getting away from home, and away from my brother even though he was in the Army most of the year, it wasn't long enough for me. The other area I felt good about was that my sexual addiction that summer left my mind after doing the work that I did while I was on the campsite.

That year my brother failed out of college, and moved back into the house for a short period. He found a girlfriend that was almost my own age. She was a stunning young blond haired, blue eyed, sex machine of a fourteen year old girlfriend that who knows what she was really like outside of her relationship with my brother, type of girl that you didn't want to bring home to you parents type of person. He brought home pictures of her naked in a shower and trying to cover her own body.

Our parents had logic to that picture taken from a different perspective. They told my brother to ask himself, who was the person on the other end of that camera. Once he started that he clearly was missing his own mother over this girl he had a crush for at the time.

That winter I was free of my brother while he went to basic training. I was especially excited to see him leave this other girl who was closer to my age than being a legally accepted age that he could have been dating.

That second year in middle school, I shared lockers with my best friend, that giant child of our elementary days, and his friend who seemed to be inseparable for most of they years before. My giant friend seemed a bit distort about our relationship and how it was going nowhere fast. I didn't expect a thing until I overheard the diabetic kid that the giant seemed to hang out with even more than I did say something about a brown leather jacket in the toilet and how he knew who had done it.

I found out that my giant friend was the one who sent my leather jacket into the seawater salute for a seventh ending stretch. I believe that the water had been used a bit prior to the flushing of the jacket though. It kept the flavor a bit longer than I wanted it to be. But all was forgiven for my giant friend. He had to pay for the dry cleaning to make things right.

I was hurt and ashamed that my best friend ruined my jacket, and even worse I made him mad at me enough to have him attempt to ruin my jacket for revenge for something that I had no idea was a problem. I am still not sure why he did that to me. It could have been for revenge or for status with his diabetic friend. The diabetic kid was constantly being reprimanded for causing trouble, and he was popular as well for a while until his morbidly obese mother was home schooling him.

She was a person that was just as sweet as her cooking, but she had a problem with diabetes and trying to lose weight. Her son and my best friend were at the other end of a ring of thieving video games that I was left un-played for days at a time. I found the labels of some of the games to still be on them from when I bought them off of a street vendor for a video game rental company.

The two of them tried to hide it, but I knew they were my games. They had been missing for some while, but I had forgotten about playing them. Then when I went to play them again they were obviously gone from my ordered list.

My best friend stood in his house, in front of his parents, and lied through his teeth about the games. He used every thing he could think of to gain status back for his problems towards his friends or other children who visited my house.

Had I taken anything away from him? Had he become so angry with me for something I did to downsize his manhood or other areas of his life? Was I ruining his popularity of a person? I felt like I had done something to make him angry towards me. Maybe I slept with his sister or something, no I didn't do that, maybe I beat up his girlfriend, and no I didn't do that. The thoughts kept going through my mind. I had no real good reason as to why he would have done that to me.

So I forgave his errors and asked him to be my friend again. Our friendship was rocky for a while with the opened can of worms for years to come. But still I wondered why he would betray trust like we had over all of those years. Maybe I would never find out, or maybe I would and it wouldn't matter anyway because I loved him too much for who he was, a poor boy with very little in his life. He had everything that I wished I had in my own life. Namely I wanted a younger sister to be friends with versus an older brother who raped me everyday.

My giant friend and I were drawing further apart as the year went on. All that I thought about was how much he had hurt me and I constantly worried about what I did to make him hate me so much. The pastor at my church told me to pray about it.

I wasn't into prayer. What good would that do me if it was a physical thing, its not something I wanted God to solve after all he had much bigger things to deal with than me. The giant boy did pay for my jacket to be cleaned, but that was more punishment than a kind jester of friendship.

It felt like I was being punished for keeping my sex life a secret from my parents. It was as if I lost a good friend to something so simple that if I thought hard enough I would have the answer. The feeling of being lost and alone kept coming over me and God was busy with larger issues of my father's health. In any case my friends decision was to be the way he was at that time and so I had been powerless over my friends decision. It was not that I wanted to lose him as a friend, but it was like losing my real brother and being stuck with an imposer that abused me profusely.

My father was in and out of hospitals that year. He lived in hospitals for two years straight and it was hard to visit him as he was in and out of surgeries that were so life threatening that a doctor's office actually put his files into the death records because the issues he had were so dire that his chances of surviving the surgery were less than five percent. He had Pancreantitus.

This was only the first of the many years he would have to live in a hospital bed. He spent over six months in Iowa City where he was holding at a 104-degree temperature. The end of the surgery left him with a huge scar like a sad face across his stomach that was fourteen inches across by about 3 to 5 inches wide in spots.

The doctors kept his wound open to heal from the inside out and this made it easier to get back in if they had to do any further emergency procedures. His nurses and interns at the hospital in Iowa City first performed the packing of gauze, but then it had to be done at home by my mother or myself.

The surgery took what seemed like hours of time. He was out for over 12 hours and he was over bearing with infections and pain. He was taking volumes of morphine and Tylenol at large increments. He didn't eat for 5 of those six months. He drank water and was fed through IV's. He had a catheter in both ends because they didn't want him to move and pull out staples or the wire mesh that held his internal organs back from falling out. My favorite game at the time was "Mortal Kombat", and that game had nothing over on my father's scars and seeing his stomach from a top view. How he was still alive I don't know and neither do the doctors really, but God had answered my prayers for my father to continue living.

So at that time I believed that my answer was correct. I had to save my prayers for bigger things than my problems. My prayers saved my father from dying. That's what the doctors told my mother and I, and that's what I believed as well. How else could I explain it to people? It was a miracle at its best.

Back in school my life was more lost than ever. I was again doing poorly in all of my classes except for music. My teachers were very sympathetic to a point, but they didn't even begin to understand the hell that I was being put through. No one could have, and I took it in short strides. I had to I was short.

I had no real close friends due to my absence from school for so long. I waited for things to settle down with the giant friend. He would apologize to me profusely and then he gave me a hug that he was so good at giving. I learned as much as I could while I was worried about my father and his health going up and down. I also knew that causing trouble over being good got me more of the attention I needed, even if it was bad attention. It seemed to bring the girls around me a little bit more. Plus they were all being sympathetic towards my situation with my father in the hospital.

I was always opening my mouth further to gain more publicity to turn away anyone who thought I was sane. The actions I took towards others often led my body to be a potential punching bag, but lucky for me I started having more and more friends back me up due to my father's illness. So I took advantage of the situation fully.

I opened my mouth almost too much that year. I was trying to remove all of the crud that had been pushed down my throat from my brother and cousin's sexual abuse. It started to seem like things were going smoother than before, but then more trouble started in the realm that only God controlled. I thought for sure my father was going to die after this one.

There were floods that took over entire areas of the city we lived in back in 1993. Water was plenty, but drinking water was so scarce that we had to have it shipped in so that we could bathe or drink things. The water works plant was underwater; flooding caused drinkable waters to become contaminated and unusable for anything other than flushing the stool. My father needed the water to clean his huge scar on his belly and keep it infection free. This made things even more challenging for him as he was forced to return to work that summer of the flood after being off of work for almost a years time.

The floods ended residing back into the river leaving chaos across the city. Busses floated away down the river, garbage and debris showed it's ugly face after being waterlogged for several weeks. Volunteers were needed very much for cleanup and for handing out water to those who were still without. My giant friend and I volunteered to hand out crates of milk jugs by the gallons at the local dairy truck depot.

All of this good work was being done by a child who, just weeks before, almost got a bus driver fired for his own stupid lies. Various children were tormenting me on my school bus and so I found friends, well so called friends, to walk home with me from school one evening. We stopped at a local multi-purpose shop and played video games and caused a ruckus at the stores demise. I left without them thankfully as they left with a ride to somewhere I wasn't about to go. Jail was in there future, and home was in mine. So I left the story and hurried home before I got into even more trouble.

I told everyone at home that the bus had broken down in the suburbs and I walked home from the back roads because I didn't want to wait for the bus to get fixed. Not thinking of my parent's worries about me, they called the bus driver into a meeting with my parents and found out the truth about the whole ordeal and I was again grounded from seeing these so called friends ever again. Well I was ok with that because I don't think that they would have been much fun being joined in jail by my addicted personality.

The next several bus rides were very harsh and prone to bringing me more and more pain. I would have things thrown at me; I would have people screaming that I was a liar, and a thief. I didn't know what else to say other than "shut up!" Even that was less than I deserved though. I would continue to break rules, but I found that riding the city bus was a little bit easier for me in the long haul of things.

One thing that made my life hard to deal with in school after that was the healing process of the beating, that the boy who reminded me of Charlie Sheen, that took place months before this incident was now causing my nose to bleed huge clots of blood and infectious packets that the blood held back from my brain.

Body was fighting back at me for all of the abuse I caused it over the past several years. I was getting kidney infections from the over usage of my penis. I was getting bruised easier and with more frequency. The soap opera at church wasn't helping matters and people were more worried about my father than about me. I was always second to my father's care. I was always left out in the cold when it came to things unseen.

I was becoming more and more selfish by the day as people directed their focus on other people and I closed my self off from the world because of how cruel it had become to me. I was truly a shadow of my own design at this point. Hidden in my room for hours either eating, studying, or sleeping, I kept my doors locked from anyone entering including my parents.

My actions were excaudate by my thoughts and dreams. I was masturbating all the time, and even in my sleep. I couldn't go anywhere without first looking at a pornographic magazine or some form of erotic fantasy video. It was my only comforter in the times where I was alone. But I was alone what felt like all times of the day. And with others being cruel towards my feelings and towards how I looked or dressed it made it all the more horrifying to live out my life.

That same year I started Tae Kwon Do to help defend myself against those bully-types. I went twice a week for the remainder of that school year. It was easy for me to be there it was at the hospital where I knew the people very well.

I still bowled, took piano lessons, and I started Tae Kwon Do later in the game, but it was Tae Kwon Do that took up most of my time. In those classes I met up with several new friends, and I also helped bring in some of my own friends.

One of the families that were teaching the class had five kids alone. They were the class in it's self. If they were gone it was left down to about ten other people. The oldest was a young man who reminded me of a young Chuck Norris, but then he had a sister that reminded me that I was a sex addict that wanted his sister. I think that she had a crush on me as well.

If not she lied for me very well as I told others that we were dating as a couple. She sparred with me for the efforts of getting close and allowing me to rub up against her. I stayed the night at their house a couple of times and I wanted to keep up the ruckus of being there, but for some reason I was only able to the two times. She did come out for breakfast with no underwear on and that fed my addictive behavior even more than the sparring.

At first glance I wasn't sure how to take her. Was she flirting or was she just forgetting that she had a guest there and always dressed down. The problem I had was that I wanted more than just her word on the event; I wanted to see as well. I knew I couldn't, but I wanted to.

I had learned a lot of useful life lessons from their father's teachings and I was left speechless a time or two, as they would constantly bring my life up to speed with the rest of the world. I was amazed at the effort that they brought to my table to get me straightened out. But it was of no avail as their father's wife finding love with another man split the family up and forced their father to live single man's life in depression for years. After that he was never again the same happy person he was with his family. Then again I don't know who would be after such a surprise end.

Chapter 8

Finally!!!?

How could I have passed the seventh grade year? I was getting my butt kicked by everyone who wasn't a friend and many more that were. I think the hitting again affected my brain from functioning fully. I became quiet and shy towards everyone. I was the quiet, shy, hidden guy, weak, unique, computer geek, and I had a fetish for music.

That year I became a pushover for girls in my class, as they would woo me into about anything they wanted me to do. I spoke with girls and they acknowledged me from a distance. I was feeling pretty much the same as before. Except that I became close to God that year after my father went through so much pain and lived.

I wasn't sure why God would love me? God had a different plan for me I knew for sure, but I didn't think that it would involve groping girls as I went down the hallways of my junior high school. I would try to not think of sexual thoughts throughout the day as they came and went. I think that actually made the problems worse.

That summer I spent most of my days inside and away from others. I had a good reason, but I wasn't going to tell them all what it was. I was too busy masturbating in my room. "Um, I have a cold and I don't feel like playing today." Did I say what I meant to say or did I just tell the truth? I couldn't remember half of the time if I was lying anymore. And the skirts on most girls were shrinking or they all used hot water to wash them in. I felt so uncomfortable around most of them that year.

That summer I really fed my addictive behavior with newer erotic items that my cousin had found under a beachfront by the river. There were hundreds of pictures in a chest. There were naked women magazines in all of them. Some pictures were worse than others, but all of them had been sexually arousing at every point of the page.

As I looked at the pages I would picture in my mind all of the girls that I was feeling like having a relationship with. The pages grew sticky from the money shots hitting the pages, as I grew more and more impatient of how long it would take me to complete my actions of sexual pleasure to various girls. Keeping in mind I was about 12 years old at the time.

That year I started swing choir and show choir. This allowed my addict to get a better feel for my fantasies in my room. I enjoyed video games all the more. And when I got bored with them I went back to the pornography and thought of various beautiful girls in my class. I had no particular type or limit to which I would have had sexual relations with in my mind. They were all great to be with, but I had special ones that would pay close attention to me in school. They had a special place in my heart at the corner of a bookcase in the yearbook.

Going back to school though meant dealing with the same rejection that I was prone to before. I found it easier to speak with girls that were in similar classes or that were in swing choir with me. But all of them were my next victims of being fondled in the hallways.

In my seventh grade year all of the girls wrote quotes in my yearbook. Many of them offered me their phones numbers with a sexually explicit comment about how they wanted to do some form of sexual act on me. How did they know so much about sexual acts I don't really know, but I was turned on by the whole situation? All the girls in real-life situations would reject me, but in my fantasy I could have any woman I wanted.

The girls in my class would tease me sexually; they flirted with my penis through my jeans, and shut me down when I was about to ask them for sex. It was their way of getting even with me for touching them in the hallways. It felt like I had at least a little bit of a chance, but it was also a cruel thing to tease me the way that they did. I couldn't tell if they were serious or if they were actually playing the part and getting me into more trouble.

One of my other close friends told me that those girls who gave me their numbers were playing me. They wanted to get a reaction out from me for the negative outcome of shutting me down. What a cruel way to treat a person I thought as I passed those same girls in the hallways. I knew they didn't know what they were missing out on. It was in my mind as sexual interaction for hours on end, and a love over that person that would be unmatched by any other guy in the area. It was no wonder why other girls were pregnant at that time.

Acting like a sexual dog wasn't going to get the women to like me, but for some guys in my classes it seemed like that was all they had to do was ask. It was like they were the sexually experienced people and I was nothing more than trash. This caused me to become deeper into my fantasy world causing more harm than good to my behaviors, and I was feeling lost and alone again. I was like a horny dog. I tried to hump any one's leg I could find and some with out legs as well.

By the time I reached puberty, I was already having sex with myself over 5 times a day. I had to be good in bed if I could last that long, after all I knew myself better than any woman I could have slept with.

My eighth grade year was also the year I had to make choices in extra-curricular activities. Did I want to keep playing the piano, did I want to lose my Tae Kwon Do class as an option, or did I want to remove bowling. I chose to give up piano and bowling because I didn't get to touch girls at either of them items. But while I was still in a league, I did manage to step into the arcade a time or two and catch a girl in a skirt and I would play with her as she played a game.

I found out about my brother's new girlfriend a few months before all of this went down. She was a very nice blond girl with two chins, but she was skinny. It was weird at first, but she grew on me very quickly along with her son who was only three at the time I first met the two of them. My brothers' girlfriend would later marry him and her son would become my step nephew and I would molest him at about 6 years old. Like my brother was with me, I was 8 years older than my nephew was. It was a repeated cycle of events that were inevitable to occur for both my new founded nephew and myself.

He came up with the whole idea himself. He mentioned that he knew what sex was and that he and a friend of his were sexually playing with each other at night. So I told him I used to do that with my brother, and thinking it was a good way to better know him we had a one-time relationship with each other in bed. But I didn't want to stop there with him; because he was so open about it and yet very quiet about it as well that I couldn't believe he had even mentioned it to me in the first place.

I was a bit excited that I could have someone to share this deep hidden secret with and someone again I could love sexually in our spare time. I often found myself falling asleep and masturbating while I dozed off.

I am not sure if I did anything else in my sleep such as attempt to have sex with friends that stayed over or not, but I was always sleepwalking and I found myself in weird predicaments all of the time. I fondled a cousin in my sleep that wasn't normally a part of the group of cousins having sex, I found myself attempting to have sex with my new found nephew at night when he stayed at my parents house when I was a 12 year old boy.

My brother was about 20 years old when he had first met his future wife. They hit it off pretty good and she was just rid of another man she had been married to for five years of hell. He had gotten into an accident and amazing enough three girlfriends appeared at his hospital bed along with his wife. She signed the papers for a divorce the next day and took her son with her and never looked back for a very long time.

That year I wanted to make people pay for what they said and did to me over the past several years. I purchased a stink bomb and showed it off not thinking someone else would take it and smash it in the room for me. There was a heavy girl that talked like she was the queen of the world she was living in and she told the world that her crap didn't stink. So I wanted to prove her wrong with the stink bomb.

My teacher in English class that year was a white haired; old prune of a woman, with a q-tip for hair, and a love for Hitler the Nazi Governor of Germany. Yep, she was amazed at his generous and how well he lead Germany to victory after victory and how his medical practices brought in various cures to illnesses in other people since they practiced on Jews. Such a kind, and wonderful teacher in a public school she was. Not really, she was one of the rudest women I had ever met up with. I despised her tact towards boys in her class and how she treated everyone differently as either favorites or as peons that weren't worth the spit to send them flying across the room.

She had a colorful way of looking at people, as long as you looked black or white she was seeing everything in color. She was prejudice towards minorities and men. She discriminated against me when the stink bomb went off and forced me to sit in the smell of it because the class sided with the two culprits that actually set it off. I was guilty of purchasing the bomb from a friend and showing it off, but not of breaking the glass. I had to defend my pride against the giant hippopotamus of a girl that dared to call me fat. She was bigger than me. She was at least twice the size of everyone else in the school. And her only insult was that I was a nerd and a fat one at that. Maybe she was mad because I didn't dream of her? I did that night and for about a week straight after that experience.

I practiced what I would do to her nightly on my stuffed animals and their intestines (stuffing). I wasn't actually going to hurt a human being with the problem, besides she would beat me up, or sit on me.

That was how I thought out logic at that grade level. I didn't want to even mention that I would have done that with most of my touching victims if they had told anyone I did it with them. I really couldn't, but I would have told them I was going to if they told. It was that action of events that got me suspended from school for my first time ever. But there was still more of that year to deal with.

My giant friend would constantly tell me about a day of the week right before the end of the school year when students in the eighth grade year could jip out of class to go freely wonder the halls or outside of the school. Somehow I talked him into skipping classes with me that day.

We walked all over the east side of the school for about an hour or two, when we happened upon two younger boys than us.

The kids mocked us and told us to return to school. Their mother home schooled them. That was what they shouted at us as they chucked rocks our direction. Several hit around us, but one hit my giant friend in the head. He began to cry and started walking away from them in tears. I turned and followed my friend hoping to get him to help me beat the two little hoodlums back into their house, but all he could do was cry and blame me for coning him into going out for eighth-grade jip day.

He snuck back into the school where the classes were just letting out for the fifth period of the day. There he snuck into the crowded hallways and left me to fend for myself.

Shortly after that jip day, we had a gym class outside where we played various games of dodge ball hopscotch, and jump rope. In all of the fun we were having the same bully from my seventh grade year that accused me of picking my nose attempted to pull my pants down and de-pants me in front of all of my piers. I turned around and with a quick jerk de-pants'ed him instead. He was then pulled into the principals' office for misconduct and for flashing his genitals at girls in public.

Getting into the swing choir that year meant that I was at the top of the game in music. It also helped my addiction become more opened and visually appealing to me. But like all good things in an addicts mind, they all must end.

The year was ending and I was alone without having been involved in the last parts of the shows.

Our music teacher as beautiful as she was up there was more stunning than ever. I cried because I was going to miss her hugs and her singing. The music of the choir was awesome, and then the lights came back on for the stage. We all chipped in and got her a present to say good bye forever unless we would stop back and visit, but we were with her at school what seemed like days at a time practicing and rehearsing parts of our show.

So to make things flow more smoothly we made her a huge card and we all offered our condolences and cleaned the auditorium and organized her room for her as best we could.

Then with several tears, and a huge hug from our teacher we were all gone for the evening, and I cried for hours due to the loss of a great teacher that I would miss for years to come.

The last week of school, we had tryouts for choirs at our high school of choice. I made the top-level choir at my high school the first time through. And little did I know how much that would have affected my musical career as a student or as a professional musician.

Chapter 9

Not so freshmen

It was the summer of my 9th grade year at my local high school. That year I made a lot of enemies and a lot of friends, but I don't recall too much after that. That would be mostly due to the dream that I had woken up from after hearing I was chosen to be in the highest level of choir at my new high school.

In trying out I sounded awesome according to the director. He was a tall slender brown-haired man with glasses, and a reputation for gathering several choir champions. For me this was an honor to be picked. I couldn't imagine conflicts it would have caused at that point.

Students that were previously chosen by our junior high school teacher were dropped down into lower choir levels and I for some reason was brought up out of the heap of trash that I was being called all of those years to perform with the top of the class choir students.

I only knew the instructor for that day of tryouts, and I must have really impressed him with my talents no other students from any other schools made the cut that year. I was overwhelmed with joy.

Later I was told how good I sounded to the instructor. My junior high teacher said that I was one of four out of two hundred male vocalists that tried out and made the top of the choirs. My dreams seemed to be coming true for my musical career. I wanted to sing for thousands of people and this would be my chance.

The problem with that though was that I was afraid to perform in front of people of a large number. I was especially nervous in performing solos. As a child I was a showboat performer, but as a teenager it was a different story. I realized what embarrassing moments awaited my future. That was one excuse, and the other was that my brother was multi-talented in playing instruments. He was able to play drums, trumpet, and saxophone. He was best at the trumpet.

I love to say that my instrument was my voice, but my brother was jealous of me every time I sang in the house. At times I think that my brother resented me a lot for my voice. But I was also a very vane singer. I used my voice to impress his friends. My pride that year was very much in vane.

I started out my freshman year at high school with a huge head on my shoulders. Some said I had a bigger head on my shoulders than the school could hold, but I ignored them they were just jealous of my natural talents. I still don't know how my head fit through the front doors.

The weird part about being one of the only four students being picked for the highest-level choir at the school was that the same four male vocalists who were the best at our junior high school were the same at our high school. We were all four good friends, and we all sang in the same choirs together.

I remember having dreams about becoming a big star later on in life. I dreamed of becoming a rock star like "Bonjovi." But the fact remained that it would take a lot of hard work and effort to get to that high of status. For my own dysfunctional benefit I was impatient and I didn't want to wait for perfection. So I didn't really try hard at it for the fact that my parents said it would be too hard to become a musical celebrity.

That year my life felt like it was starting for the first time. I got to the top of the chorus' classes in a single vote, I was starting to get good at my Tae Kwon Do, and the summer with the youth group that I was in was amazing as well that year. What was so great about that summer at church camp?

It had to be the number of cute young girls on my watch that all flirted with everyone except for me of course. I was always alone at those campsites. I took several friends with me that year, and I was still all alone as they all went off to play football or "Ditch the dork". I did manage to race the vehicles down the hill to the work sites where we all learned how to paint a windowsill, build a log cabin, and perform chores. But I was more interested in trying to play on the girls.

I hit on every girl at the camp that summer, and I didn't even get a single maybe. Rejection was my calling for the longest time. It didn't matter how much more courageous I was than other people. They would call me stupid for helping the women get through obstacles in the paths. If someone else did it though they would thank him or her and possibly give him or her a kiss or a hug.

Her boyfriend was dragging one girl out of camp when she told him to get lost. I overheard the conversation along with the rest of the campsite, and anyone else within yelling distance. She was beautiful on the outside, but on the inside she was brutally a witch, and a total user of a woman. If it wasn't for her outer beauty I don't think that she could have found a date with anyone even if she begged.

Then again, for some reason the girls at camp seemed to have something that all the other guys were attracted to. Beer flavored nipples? Nah! It was a worse than normal nightmare for me. I wanted at least one of them to acknowledge me, but I was too nerdy to be of any sort of boyfriend to these ladies. Plus I had a thing with touching the other women in the group and they all knew it, but none of them seemed to mind either, as I never got into any trouble over it.

The two clowns that were also hitting on the other women were having more success than I was because they were bigger than me. They dressed better, they had larger wallets than I did, and they had looks of men and not of a nerdy little boy. I didn't understand why the girls liked them; those two were more like a married couple of girls than any other person I knew.

The first one was a tall skinny blond, preppy boy, who loved to use women to get into bed with them. He used women like paper-towels and threw them away like them as well. But he had one girl that would keep going in and out of his life. She babied him to the ends of the world, and she taught him how to dress and become popular for her sake.

The second one was a tall toad of a man. He had black curly hair, baby blue eyes, and a nasty temper for hurting others. He also seemed like he was afraid of certain people in his life like I was, but that didn't matter to me, he was hitting on the women I wanted to hit on.

They were both considered bad boys in the group. The girls seemed to like the bad boy image that each one of them took out when the girls weren't looking. Behind the scenes they were girlier than most supermodels about their hygiene and beauty tips. They pampered their own nails and they had to have perfect hairstyles to match their attire. Both of them were best friends, but they also had egos that clashed with each other like "the three stooges".

Both of these boys were women users, but different from what I was. The blond airhead of a man was tall, slender, and a political con man. The other boy was a tall heavy, burly young man with bright blue eyes, and his curly black hair with the G-curl going into fashion. He was the type that was a tough guy and a brawler of a man. Both were so manly in their mannerisms that they reeked of man-hood. They also hid their emotions and true feelings behind a huge facade of smoke, mirrors, and beauty techniques. I found this out much later in the school year after meeting one of my best friends of all times in high school.

With all of this going down at the campsite it was hard to believe at first that the people I was involved with at church would end up being a part of my high school days as well, with one exception of the fat, black-haired, girly-man previously mentioned. This is where my high school story really starts to kick off.

The first day of choir practice happened to be right after camp and right before the school year started out. Little did I know that I would be taken for a ride on a bus with the very same girl that would be the blond boy's ex-girlfriend? I received a call from an unknown voice. I was told to meet up at the high school at about 6:30 AM to begin practicing and breaking of the ice as well.

I was extremely excited to go, and I arranged for myself a bus ride to make it to school on time. Getting up at 5:00 AM that morning meant having a commitment to a schedule and I was not about schedules as of yet, but I was very willing to try. When I got on the bus I spotted to really relaxed and excited girls that were apparently not much older than I was, but I wasn't about to say anything.

So I dreamed of what I would have done to them with my fantasy worldview of things.

The first girl was a short-stocky blond with curly hair, and she was obnoxious about everything she talked about. She reminded me more of a man than a woman. I felt like I knew the other one from somewhere though? She was built to be a woman of any mans dreams. She had beautiful brown hair, brown eyes, and a very curvy body that you would want to drive on and take it for a spin and never go back. I had to know who she was and I had to get to know her if I could.

The short blond one was a dunce of a woman who at first glance, you might have thought that she was a clown, but then realizes that she was just a blond. "No offense to the one's who are smart." I walked over to them and asked if they too were up this early for choir practice. Of course they were and I was very excited to know that I wasn't the only one riding the bus to practice that morning. Being the gentleman I was I let the ladies go first? "Now ladies if you are reading this, just because a man lets you go first doesn't mean he is a gentleman. He is probably checking your butt out! Look back at men sometime. If they are looking down this is what they are actually staring at! That is unless they are married! Then they are looking for loose change." Getting back to the story, I found myself looking at the brunette's figure all of the way to the school. I felt so lucky to be in this choir that I thought I was going to through up from all of the excitement.

I don't recall if I could even speak to the Goddess as she walked down the sidewalk and into the school. I walked about 20 feet behind them as they talked about the previous school year and the previous director, and what they thought the new director would be like.

All I could think of was, how I was going to put my moves on the hottest girl I had ever seen in my life and especially if she was single. No man deserved her, not even me. But I was bound and determined to try. So I decided to hand out in the choir room and hoped that she would notice me. The very same day, it was like a prayer had spoken down from God as she actually talked to me for the first time. I just about threw up on my shoes, with the belched out "hello!" greeting I felt my heart explode from the pressure I was under. Regaining my poise, I didn't really know how to act around her. She was a bitch to everyone, but me. Not sure why that was, but I think that she just had a likeness for a hateful mind or me for those who she had already known to be rude to her.

Rule number 1: Don't get on super hot chick's bad side. "Got it!" As the plans to woo her became clear to me, I was about to embark on a journey of four years to make her mine. Only to fail time and time again, mostly due to my scared look, and the fact that I didn't want to harass her to the point of her wanting to leave me in the dust as she ran off.

I remember being told by the dumb jock-boys in the locker rooms I was gay and a sissy for being in the choir instead of playing sports like they were. Now think to yourself for a moment here gentlemen.

If I am around a bunch of women my whole day through helping them perform lifts, and other acrobatic acts, who exactly is getting all of the action? That usually shut most of them up for about a minute to think about it. The only comeback I ever heard from most of them was, "Well we have the cheerleaders!" My only response was, "Well, you need them!"

I considered myself very lucky and privileged to have such an eyeful of women around me constantly and being able to dance and sing with them was an honor. In fact in my mind, I could take a woman home with me every night and pleasure her for hours in my mind. The fantasy was so real to me it was better than most women. I wasn't rejected, turned away, ugly, or too innocent. In my mind I was the best of everything sexual and I knew it. In reality I couldn't even begin to prove it, but I had always wanted to, and sometimes I still do. But I was truly becoming an addict of my own thoughts and dreams.

Girl after girl of rejections, I chose to fondle my women when they didn't know I was. But I was never satisfied by my fantasies enough to replace the real deal with women. Then we became friends. The "We" was that hot brunette girl that was ahead of me during that long walk to the high school for that first practice.

We drew closer as friends, but I seemed to not care about our friendship, I for some reason seemed to want more. I had overheard several conversations about her from her ex-boyfriend who still wanted to be with her and how he was going to try and lay the moves down. I would warn her of his presence and I would help her to stay away from the scum of the earthman he was.

There were too many times I saw her get hurt in the past months by jerks. I couldn't be asking her now, could I? So, I waited for her to become absent of the other men in her life, which seemed to be never. She wasn't sleazy or a flirt, but she was an honest hardworking girl that I felt was the only girl in the world that treated me halfway like a human being. I watched her waste a long time with him only to have her heart broken too many times. I sat in those stairwells holding back tears to have my chance to be with the girl of my dreams.

I felt like the ugly gay boyfriend, whom always gave advice, but never bothered getting in with the girl. The problem with that scenario was that I wasn't gay, and I didn't think I was ugly, but I felt like something was wrong with me as I wasn't getting sexed up like I was before. It made me feel unattractive and I grew more ashamed of my appearance and my status in life. I was becoming the lost soul in the crowd of people that everyone passes by and never attempts to help even though they were crying for someone to help.

That year I didn't feel attractive, I didn't feel happy, and I felt like I didn't have feelings anymore. I would just smile and act as other people did in those times of good days. I hid my lies and emotions very well and I lied a lot to keep my secret hidden that I was actually thinking of sexual thoughts about everyone else because I knew it wasn't normal for anyone to think that way, or so I thought.

I tried to gain affection and love the only way I knew how. That was through touching women and brushing up against them or asking for hugs rather than a handshake. I crept many girls out with my actions and words. I had no morals, and I had no boundaries for wanting what I wanted. I think I was the only one in school brought up on sexual harassment charges to get off Scot-free and continually be brought back into offices for problems constantly. I counted at least 20 times for the same thing.

I started realizing I was taking dangerous roads to the bad side of the issue. I was becoming like my older brother and I was thinking of what he did to me, and how I could do it to other people. That seemed logically how I had to get sex from then on. I had to take it like everyone else did. It made sense to me. Logic was twisted in a huge mesh of lies and deceit. And I was at the middle of the puzzle trying to untangle the web I was dropped into from the beginning. The first thing I learned was to mimic the people around me, and then pretend to know everything about the subject matter that they were talking about. I was intelligent in books, but when it came to people I had no clue. I was becoming my brother, the abuser.

My younger nephew would come to me on occasion and ask me to perform sex on him as practice. I agreed at first, but then it started to remind me of my brother's torturing techniques he performed on me. He was about five or six years old at the time, and I was no more than thirteen. It felt like love to me. That was how everyone else in my family showed me love behind closed doors.

I asked my nephew where he learned how to perform this type of interaction, and all he could tell me was with a friend. I asked him if it was my brother, but he stopped the conversation there and stopped the sex. I chose to continue without him, and then I got up out of bed and we began playing videogames just as my brother walked through the door to check up on us. I could see the fear in my nephew's eyes as he looked at my brother. I could tell right then that he had been taking my place in his abuse battles with my brother. I didn't say anything because I thought that after the Army my brother had changed for the better, but it made the rage even more brutal and lethal.

All of morality had left my mind and I was an animal in a young man's body. My mind and feelings of love left me at the sideline of life. I was drained of all love and affection by the years of abusive behaviors that were performed on me, and I was performing these acts on other people to a point. I would stop myself short of having sex or abusing them. I became a peeper of sorts. I didn't want to harm people. I wasn't like my brother who was evil in hurting others and getting his way all the time.

While I had been working this angle before, I was performing these actual areas of sexual immorality with my cousins for years. I eventually stopped myself from harming myself multiple times after being rejected so often. A person with a heart can only take so much rejection until they cannot function anymore. Our hearts are controlled by our minds, and if our mind goes, so does the heart.

One day I was talking with my sister-in-law about my brother and the way he was acting around my nephew. To hear what my brother was doing to my nephew, it all seemed mild and loving compared to what I endured over the years with him.

To reiterate my story of my brother further, he was the type of person, who was a Jekyll and Hyde type of character, and he could fool anyone with his lies and aggression was lost to him at the drop of a hat. It was this training I received from my brother that got me to where I was then, and I even fooled the master of the problem, my brother. The only exemption to the rule was when he caught me in the lie; I would end up cowering in a corner of the room. He would let me go for about ten seconds and then he would allow me to get to the steps and then pull my legs from under me and force my head into the steps and drag my body like a doll down the stairs.

The one time I stepped up to face my brother I aimed high, kicking him in the genitals and watched as he dropped quickly to the ground. I attempted to run away only to have him grab my leg as I began to run. I soon after that fell on my face knocking a baby tooth loose and causing me to bite my lip.

Conflicts at school were nothing compared to his brutality towards me, but they were still present. I never got into a fight, but I had a lot of enemies that wanted to fight me. I was too fast for them. They didn't expect a fat kid to run so fast, but I could out run them all and hide quickly into other rooms.

I ran into the choir room several times to save my skin and be greeted by our new choir teacher of those years experience. It wasn't the man I tried out with; however, it was almost the opposite of the man to the letter.

She was a short, frail, boney, blond, mother of three children, and an attractive woman for being over fifty years old. I wanted my wife to look that good at fifty. She was also a Jazz musician, and recording artists as a back story all of its own.

With the old teacher gone and the new lady teacher in place of such a great director that the previous teacher was, we were all stressed out about the changes that were made without a second opinion. The students who were there the entire time a year before the four of us arrived were leery at best to have four nerdy looking singers in their crisp, clean-cut, grooving to the music group of beautiful people, and they were an out-right egotistic group of individuals with no morals to spin out of either end of the space of time.

With this group of ruffians I felt more comfortable being around the jocks at this point. On my first impression, I was gathering that I should be by myself in a corner alone and away from everyone else. I kept my feelings tucked away and made up stories of pity and self worth that was way out of this lifetime for someone like me, but I was believable about it. I kept telling folks I was 15 or 16 years old when I was fourteen. I would tell them that the reason I was so short was due to my birth defects and genetic composition of my parents and how they were around me. I felt alienated by most of them until I told them I was orphaned at one time until my parents came back and got me and brought me back home. Again, I did just about anything to gain attention and try to fit into this world I didn't know existed.

As I sat in the corner of the risers that were more like chairs that we stood on, I was greeted by the same girl I was lusting over as I walked into the school earlier that morning, she came over and sat down next to me and popped my personal bubble space that I had set around myself from the germs of the other negative thinkers of the group. She began by introducing herself and several of her friends that were in the group.

Slowly things started to calm down and people would begin to come together and sing. The first time we sang it was horrible, but beautiful. I couldn't read sheet music, to save my own skin, but I learned very quickly about how to read it and play it on the piano that year. Most of it I played by ear and listened for the correct note.

The verbiage of each student was very widespread and I couldn't understand their terminology of certain words, as I was isolated from people for so long. I eventually caught on to most of the terms. The brunette and I got very close and intimate in a level I had never experienced before. It seemed what was like loving a person without being sexual. It was everything I wanted and with out having sexual intercourse with another person. It felt like something that I had been missing, but was it love or was it the fact that she was hugging me and crying on my shoulder. I embraced her close as her tears filled the corner of my shirt. I was really glad to be there for her as she was ruined for some reason or another. I didn't pay any attention to that I was being touched and held, granted negatively, by a girl I had a crush on. And she was coming to me for advice.

She and a couple other students would become my family that year. We all drew close to each other and we all became inseparable. While it wasn't quite what I had in mind that love was, I felt loved by their presence, and I was very much a part of the group for the rest of that year.

To illustrate the faith in love that we all had, we ate together, shared stories about our lives with one another, and even dressed ourselves in front of each other to get the job done. We had to in order to get ourselves ready at performances. We didn't have time to look back and notice someone didn't have underwear on or that the bra strap was loose. This kind of relationship of dressing in front of each other became the norm, and we were all cool with it after several performances.

This type of behavior was common to be around. No one ever saw each other get dressed because they were too busy dressing themselves. The stage would be packed full of flailing clothes and people running to get them on. It was like you would see in a Las Vegas style of movie where the dancers and actors are back stage get ready for the next scene. But there was a huge amount of work that needed to be put in before the performances. This was where I was the worst addictive behavior. The shows were more of a professional sense of accomplishment.

Preparing for these shows included many hours of practice and struggles to hold a note while lifting up people, moving around on stage while keeping in pitch, and performing acrobatics while holding a high note at times. But even this was not as important to most of us as the All-state Choir tryouts.

All-state was the very first major competition where only the best of the best singers are put through a gauntlet of judges and either given the opportunity to tryout again, or if they were good enough they were selected to be a part of the All-state choir.

Practice for this choir took two months to prepare for. Not that we didn't need more time, but it was very difficult music. The music found in this statute was very crisp if performed correctly, but very detrimental if a note was off by even the slightest bit.

Hour after hour, day after day, we practiced at all hours to get the songs right. In our own minds sleep even came second to practicing for a spot at the All-state choir. If we were at school at 6 AM we would leave school at 4 PM each day. Sometimes we would have all-night practice sessions.

Our voices took hits daily as we prepared for the long winded, short 15 bars of a song that was sung in a foreign language.

A lot of the songs were in Latin or Hebrew. We also had the Battle Hymn of the Republic to sing as part of our heritage environment each year. It was that song that was like the star spangled banner of the baseball world.

We practiced with colds, fevers, and broken bones. Many times we were sleep deprived, but I know I loved the work and the sound we were making with the music we were given. These guys and gals were becoming my family more so than the people I lived with at home.

So much of my time in high school was spent singing in the choir room that it felt like I did live there! I don't know why I wouldn't have thought of more things than music, but I could only think of one other thing than music, and I was embarrassed to think about that. I dreamed about that at my so-called home.

I became so obsessed with the girls in the choir I became an addictive mind when I sat in my orange chair, to the point of chaffing my penis and body parts raw. My voice after practicing at choir was just about as bad though. I did manage to sleep on occasion when I had to stay at a hospital with my father.

My home life that year wasn't much better than putting myself into a hole in the wall and hiding. Even that would have been more fun and it probably would have given me a feeling of accomplishment.

In school I had to lie to teachers and students about how I felt. I was living life to its emptiest. I felt like I had to lie to everyone to be a part of the conversation otherwise I was left out. My height, weight, and pale complexion were to blame for a lot of my self-demoralization and loser lifestyle I ended up living in.

I began touching women in inappropriate ways. Many times I would lift up a skirt or touch a breast of one of the girls and make it seem like an accident. Many of them caught on after a while of it. I was glad every year there was new subject to fondle.

I didn't feel loved by people because I wasn't getting sex from them. This was how I felt people really loved me. I wasn't aware in my own mind that people didn't want sexual activity all of the time, but I could see that they didn't want it, so I pretended to be the same thing as they were. I mimicked their movements, their words, and their relationships. I became my own puppet of sorts. Although I had my own personality no one in high school ever got to see it. I was afraid that if they did I would be isolated even worse than I was at that time.

One person I didn't want to know that I was some sort of freak show was the girl I wanted to be with more than any other girl, I wanted the brown haired girl from my first day at high school. She was so beautiful to me that I was blinded by all other women. She became close friends with me, but I would try and try to get her to notice my affections towards her, but she blew me off, and I was only a friend. I kept my secrets from her the most because I didn't want to lose her friendship or her feelings towards me. I wanted her to be my girlfriend, but she was too busy looking for the right guy and apparently I could never be it. I received that mentality from so many girls in high school that I felt I would not even get to be with a girl.

She was always on my mind, and I always worried about being rejected. Not that I didn't try, but I was also tired of being rejected by those who I felt a better relationship had been built with over the years. Everyone I attempted to date rejected me.

At church I would talk about her with various youth in the same grade. Little did I know that she was the girl everyone hated for some reason? She ended up telling me later that she had been a youth member before I started there, and she left due to the lack of knowledge the pastor had on the Bible for answers about simple questions. She told me about how she didn't become a full-member of the church and did so on the very last day, the day of her confirmation; she said she couldn't commit to it with God at this point in her life. She felt it wasn't the right time and she couldn't live under God's commands and not know enough about what he or she was. She had feelings of doubt about her life and about God and what God was in her life. So she said she didn't want to go through with it.

I later found out that she felt ashamed that she didn't go through with it, but then her grandmother comforted her and told her that it was the most mature move she had seen from anyone in the church. Her grandmother was more blessed that day and loved on her granddaughter for being honest and defying those people than being a liar and going through with it. She never returned to the church, except when I invited her a few more times.

As my friend I could see her inner-beauty as well as her outer beauty and I wanted to experience that with her, but God had other plans for me. My friend was a woman, and she knew how to handle her own battles. She was beautiful in every way imaginable. She was smart, loving, caring, and friendly to the core, but if you crossed her path the wrong way she was as mean and vicious as a tiger. To ask her if she was any of those she would deny all of the complements about her. Though I don't recall why, but everyone else I met that knew her in those days said the same thing I was saying.

I watched as she broke hearts of some very attractive guys by my comparison. She started with the blond ditz of a man that I will call her first x-boyfriend. I think that she used me the most, but in a good way. She would use my shoulder to cry on and I accepted that as what I was to her, a brother, a friend, and close companion, but never anything intimate like I originally wanted to be.

I once overheard her ex-boyfriend, the blond boy wonder who could do no wrong except get a girl pregnant and then turn around and deny that he ever had children of his own, and his want-to-be manly friend, the one with the jerry curls in his hair, best-friend in the world, talking about how they both slept with my brown haired beautiful friend, and how they wanted to brag that they tapped that, and how she was so good, but neither had a clue that she was a virgin. I felt silly finding out myself. I asked her out on a date, and of course she said no. I was too good of a friend to lose was her answer. I didn't know what else to say other than "Wow!!!" Then she kissed me on the cheek. Needless to say she told me never to tell anyone, and since we don't know her in this story unless you know me then you will never find out. "So, There!"

The two best friends continued their conversation until I interrupted, and told them they were full of themselves and she would never touch either one of them after I was done with telling what they were saying about doing to her. I told her everything that the two were saying about her. I was her friend and I didn't want that sort of thing to happen to her. She was an amazing person to me, and I would want her to do the same thing for me if I were in her predicament.

The way the two guys talked about her, the way they treated women was how I felt the world treated me all of those years I was being abused. I thought that this was how the world acted constantly until I met up with her and several others that year in high school.

I ended up buying her a rose and to me it was a gift in return for another gift. She seemed bothered by it and I was again ashamed at what my thoughts were of our being together. I was scared she hated me because she wouldn't date me, or that I was unattractive to the point of embarrassment. The world had done its damage to my mind at this point.

Shortly after that I made a commitment to only be there for her when she needed me. It wasn't long before that did take place. Our choir family was having all out brawls in the choir room. Two giants of men fought it out over one girl for some reason. I wasn't sure, but my friend was a part of it for some of the conversation, which consisted of very poor verbiage and women tearing clothes.

The students in my classes were rude to me. They would call me names and tell me I was a worthless piece of crap, the students said that I stunk, and I was so freaking slow that the girls swim team could beat me at chess. At this point I didn't care any more.

People were rude to me and love wasn't showing up anytime soon, so I did what any good addict does, become more addicted to what I was addicted to; sex, love, and videogames. My eldest female cousin was one that I had been attracted to after years of abuse from her.

She would get up in the middle of the night when I was staying over and she would have sex with me while I was asleep. As I would awake I would tell her to get off of me only to have her cover my mouth with her hands. I then enjoyed the ride, as I didn't want to get caught in this type of predicament.

Although I liked it, it made me feel like less of a person and more like an animal being caged up and used for entertainment purposes, but I loved to entertain. I felt like less of a person, because my only sexual interaction was with my own flesh and blood. It wasn't wanted, but I liked how it made me feel at the time, and so I stopped complaining because I was told it made me a wimpy boy to not want sex with a girl. She would continue to please herself at my expense until I started to fight back with my own form of revenge. I raped and beat her. Not hard, but I would find myself down in her room where I would take full advantage of the surprise attack she was so desperately asking for.

The weeks following those attacks I found myself at the All-state auditions. There I found many girls looming about. The idea of an addict of alcohol in a beer cooler would probably describe this image of how I felt in my mind. One young girl after another, I searched for the perfect piece of a woman's ass I could find and fondle it amongst the crowded teenagers I was with. I was very careful it wasn't someone from the group.

The girl took my hand and pushed it down as I drove my hand back under her skirt. I asked her for her phone number, I asked if she liked what I was doing to her, and I asked if I could take her somewhere private. Of course she said no, ever so silently and then unzipped my pants to the point that I could come out with my penis and play with her in the crowd of people.

That was my side of the story; the girl was probably scared out of her wits and waiting the moment to have someone come over and save her from me. My zipper was down probably because I forgot to zip it back up, and she pushed my hand down to get me away from touching her further. The hero of her hour was my own flesh and blood, my father. That particular day he was out of the hospital and cheering for his son to make it to All-state choir.

I quickly walked away as though nothing had happened. I don't know if I caused a scene. I didn't know the girl I was having sex with in the gym around a hundred people or more. I didn't know who she was and I didn't know if she liked it or not, probably not, but in my mind she did.

As I made my way through the crowds, I saw the banners come down and showing my very close friends name in the soprano's section. She had made it to the All-state choir. In fact she was the only one out of about 30 students. Although that wasn't our only competition that year, it was only the beginning.

For our bigger event trip, we went to the city of St. Louis to the Heritage Festival. While we were there we took a long tour of the city and it's attractions. The floods of 1993 took out most of what we really wanted to see, but it was still a fun time. We performed at a high school in the middle of the city. There we placed first out of two national groups that were in the same 4A grouping as we were. Not much of a competition, but we brought home the gold. The awards ceremony was at the Six Flags in St. Louis. There we had the advantage of having a fun time in the park and visiting some awesome roller coasters, thrill rides, and water rides that would get water wet. So I stood on the watering bridge and to no avail got soaking wet and ran around all day with our teacher's son and daughter.

At the awards ceremony I had to leave the kids with their father to go and be with the group. I was never more alone than I was there. I lied as I cried tears of loneliness about having a girlfriend at home, and how I missed her and I even gave her a song that they played on cue as I tried everything to get some girls attention.

Apparently, looking like you just heard your mother died wasn't good enough for this lot. Even my friend with the brown hair wouldn't dance with me. She only made a promise to and then proceeded to leave me alone in a corner to feel even more alone as I was left out of the group. Our teacher wasn't amused at how they were treating each other including me, but she was even angrier at the idea that they were being rude and ignoring everyone else in the group that had a part in the event. Only the seniors went up and got the trophies because that was what the seniors decided was the best thing to do.

Then the dance continued on without me. I never saw any of my friends from the choir that night. I stepped out alone again to look at God and tell him how cruel he was for addressing my loneliness with even more loneliness. I wished I could have died that night, but even God wouldn't grant me that honor to be possible.

The only thing I hated that night more than feeling alone, was being alone as I was feeling it too. No one danced with me that night, or even apologized for making me feel left out. They just moved on as a part of my life was crushed and burnt in a huge display of fireworks and cheering pedestrians.

That night I attempted to dance with a shadow partner as we all heard the song "Shout!" come on, which was one of the songs that we sang at the competition. Even then I felt like people were laughing at me dancing alone when I had a group of people I had just previously performed with, and none of them would even help me to not make quite as much of a fool as I did on my own.

In a photo album, I found a picture, of what was our entire group under the St. Louis arch. There I was with a fanny-pack, a crazy duck shirt, and pop-bottle glasses. I didn't know if the way I dressed actually made any difference to them or not, but I didn't care I was comfortable looking the part of a tourist in a city I was touring.

Some days in the future I looked back and thought to myself, why didn't they accept me for who I was back then. Why did I need to change to their likeness to be accepted by them? If they only knew how much I could have loved on them they would possibly have treated me differently, but I was losing in a battle for love, sex, and affection from anyone who would pay attention to the signs I was trying to give. That year I learned that you just had to love them even though you may not get loved in return. And that was how I lived my life that year and future years to come at my high school.

Chapter 10

A SOFTENED UP SOPHOMORE

You would figure someone with my expertise would have endured enough pain going through where I was as a child. As a teenager, I think it got much worse as I grew braver and more stupid. People in my life this year would make my world a living hell. Or at least I made it into a living hell and they were all in it with me.

One thing that we addicts like to do is put blame into other people's court. If we can slide past the blaming gun, then we will be left unharmed. But one thing I have learned over the years is that bullet of blame keeps going and eventually strikes the heart of everyone in a wave of patterns including the person it was originally intended for.

In my tenth grade year, I was very slow to keeping my activity schedule going. I quit playing the piano for singing, I dropped out of bowling after I bowled in a state tournament and I missed a perfect game by one pin, I managed to have my finger dislocated by a giant of an autistic kid who didn't know how to control his kicking power, and I got the same finger slammed into a car door.

The first thing I did was during the summer of that year. I was able to go to the state tournament for bowling. I was on my way up to a perfect game, all strikes. The nerves were there along with the parents whooping and hollering in the back of the crowd of people watching as I came closer and closer to a perfect game. Then it happened, my father let out a huge pale smelling gas that caused me to about hurl the ball into the other lane. If it wasn't for a lack of control that I withstood from embarrassment at that point, it couldn't have come at a worse time. His flatulence would continue to get me into trouble, even after that point.

A few weeks after that I vowed to quit bowling and never go back with my father to another bowling alley again. He didn't like bowling alleys anyway, and I didn't want the reminder of the embarrassing laughter from those who saw the event happen. So I hid like I always did. I hid away from those people who would recognize me for what happened, and I left my shame at the end of the bowling lane.

My next adventure into the hospital was when my giant friend, who was autistic and wore glasses, and I were sparing in Tae Kwon Do. We were working out very well and he got in several good hits on me. I went in for a little abnormal shots and he kicked my hand, causing the ring finger to dislocate and bend backwards. The kick took me out of the fight for good. I looked at my hand and quickly thought to myself that my finger shouldn't go that way! I snapped it back into place and watched as it swelled up like a balloon. I quickly asked my autistic giant of a friend to allow me to bow out and take a break.

I healed quickly from that injury, but a few months after that, the same finger was slammed into a car door of my parent's car. Again coming back from Tae Kwon Do, I really wanted to get inside, but as I got out of the car my mother must have been much quicker and attempted to close the door after she saw me exit the car. With my hand in position it shut causing my finger to be ripped open and start gushing blood out the palm side.

Feeling that she needed to help, my mother grabbed the first rag she could find. A soaked, dirty, gasoline filled rag that my father had been using to clean his hands off with gasoline after painting something with white paint. All of which was entering the wound as I attempted to stop the bleeding from my hand.

I was rushed to the hospital; there I received four stitches, a tetanus shot, and an angry look on my face for my mother giving me a nasty-fied towel. Bits and pieces of refuge entered the gaping hole left by the car door into my hand and ring finger. Had all of this not been for the pain of the injury, I probably would have found it all amusing like everyone else did.

But my all-time low point of high school at least for that year was attempting to have sex with the geeky girl from my first grade class. The one who reminded me of the girl from, "Dennis the Menace." I had met up with her a couple of times, and I had let her borrow a movie or two to let her be a closer friend, but she wanted more than that. So I went and dropped off the movies, and then I was invited into her house.

There she asked me questions in her skimpy outfit she had on. Which was almost nothing, and with a flick of a switch she was watching porn and getting me to give her oral sex. I then attempted to arouse myself interests, but it was no good. She was a friend and I didn't want to ruin that between us. I stopped right as I got into the inner-thigh and pulled out quickly and left even quicker than that.

Again I felt ashamed of what I had done, here I was single and I wanted to get something out of my life and I had the opportunity for it, and I could have taken the chance to have done it well, but I chose to be a moral person and let her get away. Plus she was pregnant and I didn't want to deal with that mess.

That same period of time I met my match in crazy people. Another sex addict in his own little world, and he was good at manipulating people into whatever he wanted to get from them. He was big, balding, and looked like something out of a "Popeye" cartoon. His manner towards women was very horrifying at best, and he caused more psychological harm than physical harm to most people. His sister slept with him when they were kids. And he was afraid of his sister, who was also a complete nut case of a woman with a few rocks short of a full-load.

This male character of a being, was sleeping with my nerdy friend and wound up getting her pregnant, and walking out of the relationship. I found out after I had just about slept with her, only to have him get even angrier with me for trying to.

The girl wasn't a bad looking girl, she was excellent figure for a toothpick and she had hot wavy red hair that made me sizzle for her at first. But again she was a friend and I didn't want to hurt her in any way. In further conversations with her I was asking myself why I didn't ever see such a beautiful person before that time.

Of course, the other side of me was saying, "Why the hell are you still here?" "She is naked and wanting you to have sex with her again, and she might as well feel like being a sister to you since she was dating your best friend the ogre."

That same summer I met a girl that lived next door to my grandmother. She was pretty; she had a good figure, and she didn't look like a toothpick, but she had an hourglass figure. My younger cousin and I were both head-over-heels for her, and we always had competitions to see who could get with her first. She was blond, petite, longhair, and a wild-child for most of her life.

She was beautiful on the outside, ugly on the inside, and dumber than a box filled with shipping peanuts and nothing else in the box. The one thing that made her look smart were her glasses, which I hated her wearing them, it gave a nerdy look to a not-so-nerdy woman, although when she did take them off her face she looked extremely beautiful, and I wanted that part of her.

The younger brother, of the cousin who molested me, and my other cousin as well, he would hang out with myself and this other girl. He ended up dating her where as I could never get that far because she again made up excuses for each time I asked.

She invited me over one after noon to apparently watch her take a shower and wait for my younger cousin to come home from where ever he was going. She said to me that she would be back and if he came just answer the door. About five minutes passed and she cam back up rapped in a towel no clothes on underneath. She lay down on the same couch as I was sitting and put her head opposite of me. She then said that she was going to sleep and that I should be going. I then asked her about my cousin and where he was. She said not to worry about it; she would let him know where she sent me. She then went to sleep about five seconds after she asked me to leave, but I stayed there and attempted to sleep with her and have sex with her. She about let me, but then she awoke and asked me to get out and said that I was attempting to rape her. It was the same things that happened to me with my older female cousin, the one who was the sister of my cousin who was seeing this girl.

I don't believe in making excuses for any of my own behaviors, I felt lead on by her, and she was the one who invited me down and gave me what I felt was an opportunity to be with her. She was naked from top to bottom underneath that towel, and in my mind she was asking me to have sex with her and feel her body up and down. After all no one can fall asleep in less than a minute, can they?

Having been asleep for less than a minute, I attempted to wake her up to make sure of what she was doing while I was there and she was naked. But next her body was unwinding from the towel with her help as I drew closer. I nudged her and asked her if she was awake and so I was again thinking opportunity from her to give to me. I thought to myself there is no way that she could not have been awake after a jolt of shaking her rapidly like I had just done, I would have woken anyone else up quickly including her.

As I drew closer to having sex with her, she got up and screamed at me to get out and leave her alone. She said that I was raping her and that I needed to leave. I ruined a good friendship over my addiction to sex that summer. It wasn't even fun. I wanted a relationship with a girl I loved to be around, but they all hated me for some reason or another. I can't remember why any of them wouldn't want me to be their personal boyfriend.

Shortly after the yelling stopped I ran out the door and ran home. I don't even know how I got there so fast, but I flew across the ground and never looked back to see if she was watching, or if she was chasing me.

The next several weeks of that summer, I spent with my Italian friend. He was a scrawny little ass that wanted to be the next pro basketball player. We performed dunks on his hoop at his grandparent's house where he grew up. His mother said that she was unable to take care of him, and so he would be pushed off onto his grandparents.

My Italian friend would tell me stories of how he would beat up my cousin, and sleep with my cousin's older sister. Both were probably lies, but I could confirm at least one of those myths. So I asked my cousin if she slept with my Italian friend. She responded with, "hell yeah, he was so good in bed." I couldn't believe it, but then I didn't feel so special after that moment of speaking with my cousin.

As addiction to sex and love, women are more likely to have multiple partners than men, but that is because there are more male sexual addicts than female sex addicts out in the world at about one woman to every three men. This also can cause more men to have sexual relationships with younger boys than girls. It is also quite possibly the reason for so many people becoming sexually confused at various ages. A lot of sexual addicts will usually swing both ways for a while, but then after a period of time they will definitely chose a side to stick with. Male or female are the two sides.

In sex addiction, if the abuser were female and the abused person were male, then the abused person in the subject would become gay and bias towards women in most cases. The same thing happens to females with a male abuser abusing a female person; she would become gay and have problems with men. Then there's the third part of this theory that is a bit confusing, but it is where I was as a child. I had abuse from both male and female. The problem here isn't about sex at all it is about love and who hurt the abused person the most, male or female?

For me, my older brother, and my older male cousin performed the most harm and they were the models that I wanted to set my sights on to hurt in the future. I resented men who had to have control and power over every aspect of life. This type of behavior makes a woman or group of women more uneasy around the addicted mind, that is because they speak with women on the same level as what they are thinking about and like myself, those like me have a tendency to understand women's pains better than men.

As I took a closer look at why I was becoming closer to women than men, I found myself hating men including myself. I hated the way I looked, and I hated that the women that I was around didn't like me romantically. Then there were the showers in high school for gym class.

For me it was like torture awaiting my every move. I would wait for the moment when no one else was in the shower and I was alone taking a hot shower by myself. I didn't want to compare myself with other men to see whose was the biggest one in the bunch. While I wasn't talking showers with other men, I was told I was gay because I was watching them as they all entered and exited together. Thinking to myself, "Yeah! Right! I'm the one that's gay? You all just took showers together, and probably scrubbed each others backs too?"

One day while entering the gym locker room I spotted two jocks comparing their sizes to one another. Thinking to myself again and they say I am the one who is gay? They must have their wires crossed.

My sophomore year started out with practice like the year before. We began weeks before school started to get practicing and knowing the new students. There were at least thirty new faces, but most of them I had seen before in other classes, many of them were my friends from years past. We briefly greeted each other and then we started practice as usual.

I remembered hearing one guy the year before, "I tried out and made the top choir for next year." I couldn't hold back the laughter, but he was serious. He wanted to wipe the floor with my body when he heard me say that. Then the next year came, and sure enough he was there with a lot of other students that year.

My mouth got me into more trouble again. Sure enough he was there to show me up, and be a favorite of the choir for years to come. He would be chatting with seniors and other dumb jocks, as he was one himself. He was a center for the high school team on the varsity side of the squad. Standing next to his seemed like more than enough of a humiliation, but to hear him sing was even more icing on the cake to make up for my lack of years of experience, and being lazy with my tonality.

While I came to idolize him for his kind heart and words of wisdom for others in the choir, I don't think that he really liked me much. He gave up a lot of solo spots to allow me to take on the role. I felt even worse as I wanted the part, but I also wanted the challenge to come from the people to not just let me have the role.

That year we weren't really friends, but more of acquaintances. I was in a lot of classes with him that year, but we never really talked much. I wanted to get to know him better, but he was one of the busiest people in the school. He was a very cool guy once I got to know him better and shut my mouth about the voice part of my own unraveling. He helped me stand up in conversations where I stood out of the crowd.

I had many friends in high school that were nice to me at times, but all of them had mixed feelings about me in the first place. If they only knew what I had gone through maybe things that year might have been different. I was being told that I needed to change my looks and way of thinking about the world. So I listened for a while.

One friend, I for some reason happened upon through out the previous year, seemed to take control of situations for me and lead me down a crazy and wild journey of fun and excitement. She looked like an ape, if she had more hair.

She was one of my best friends that year. But she was again a controlling factor that I couldn't really deal with at the time, but I let her attempt to make things good for me. She seemed to follow me around everywhere I went. I think that part of the reason I didn't have a date was due to her scaring them away. She had a laugh that made most male bass singers croak. But if you were on her bad side you were probably on the other end of an ass whooping you would never forget, along with pooping yourself.

One scrawny little wimp of a jock found out quickly how mean she could get. The scrawny little wimp of a boy was trying to act tough around me and said that he wasn't afraid of any one other than God himself. She took his scrawny little butt, and threw him against a locker and then she said, "So! I must me God then? Right?" To look at the fear in this poor pooping boys eyes left most people speechless, but wanting to laugh at his cowardice. I felt privileged to have my own personal bodyguard as a friend. Then she made a relationship hard to be around when I first found a girlfriend I liked.

The first part of the semester I didn't have anyone who I thought would like me for who I was, but then I met my first real girlfriend. A brunette girl, with a half-cracked smile, gapped teeth like "Madonna" and a cute set of dimples that were very sexy in my book. She was hot in her own right. That was until I found her playing around with other guys. I don't know why, but she dumped me shortly after I attempted to make passes at her in my bedroom. We kissed and I attempted to take off our clothes and have sex. She stopped me before I could ever begin to start.

I felt saddened that she didn't love me in that way. I felt so ashamed of my looks and how I was with her. We dated for two whole months, but that wasn't good enough I guess. Being sarcastic there, but I was foolish to have lost her in that fashion. But then again she turned to women shortly after dating the dumb scrawny jock boy who pooped his pants with my ape of a friend throwing him around. So, those things made me feel a little better. I at least wasn't the last person to make her want to swing that way.

That year we were like family in choir. We had our leaders, our followers, our wallflowers, and our sidekicks. I tried to forget about my past year of chaos in waiting and move on. After all, it was my turn to shine on the high school stage at the Las Vegas show. Previously, my brother took the stage by storm, and now it was my turn to really show what talent was all about.

The many years I dreamt of out performing my brother on stage seemed lost in the rubble of what was left on stage that year. The stage of his showcase was pushed back behind the curtains, dismantled, and in disarray. Instruments from bands past took over the junk piles and kept an even bigger mess of a place for us to clean if we were going to offer a Las Vegas type of show. In the back of my mind though was the idea that I was to not be like my brother with all of the mistakes and mishaps he got himself into during his high school years.

We worked hours on end to clear the stage of the old debris and make plans to build a new stage that would accommodate more than just bands or vocal choirs. We wanted to make this stage a place where all of the arts could be showcased and displayed for the high school classes to see.

One of the first things though about me being on stage and shining in front of the audiences of people, was my fear of audiences and stage fright. An instructor that was evil, conniving, and bushy white hair that stood out from the world, and outwitted those students who would fall into her evil stage of acting the part. She was as kind a soul as they came when she broke down her witty type of attitude with me one morning, I was shocked to see that she had been playing an act with others for so long that it seemed to have a believable appearance to it.

She helped me to overcome my fear of the stage, and I learned quickly as she showed me some very interesting tricks to get the audiences attention to be put onto you quickly. One thing that she taught me was to talk to people on elevators. "They hate that!" she said. "It makes them feel uncomfortable and out of their zone to deal with conversationalists," as she continued the conversation.

She talked a big game, but she was excellent at her work. I was able to lie to people and keep a straight face with the techniques that she taught to our class. Her techniques made me quiver at first test, but over a period of about ten weeks we were just as clever as she was an even getting a thing or two over on her.

It is amazing how quickly a single gesture of the hand can quickly caused uproar in a crowd of people. She raised her hand up to make a fist and pointed up with the middle finger and pointed it straight at me. She told me that my face was priceless, and that she wanted a picture of it. I was told that she used me because I looked the gentlest person in the group, or the most innocent of them all. My facial features gave way so well to her actions that she used me so much for so many demonstrations. I came back to visit her for years after that because she was so inspiring to me. She taught me a lot about how people's actions describe who they are on the inside as well as the outside.

The same thing is true, and can be said about a sex addict in a room full of people. If you send another addict in for the first one you will get him out almost one hundred percent of the time. That is because, if you are an addict, for some strange reason you will always find the other addicted person in the room no matter what other's look like, you will find them. It's just the mannerisms that we as addicts all have when we are in our addictive environment. We can smell the addict coming out to rear its ugly head.

The very first girlfriend I spoke about earlier was always sitting behind me in algebra class. There we exchanged notes, we went on three or four dates, and then I tried to have sex with her only to come up empty handed. Her response to not wanting to have sex was, "Why do men always want to play with women's breasts?" I couldn't answer her other than I found it appealing to me and I wanted them all to myself.

But shortly after that brief moment of silence I stopped and I told her that I was sorry if I was moving way too fast for her. I wanted to have sex with her, but she wanted to wait until she was much older. I agreed and we took her home.

As a sexual addict, the pain is deeply rooted into the soul; many times the addictive mind doesn't even know how to love someone over having sexual interactions with that same person. A sex addict doesn't know what love is, and they try to remove the sexual urge by masturbation to pornography for hours on end.

I cared deeply about this girl, and I attempted to show it to her by stopping what I had almost started. The next few days seemed like years as I was walking the halls ashamed of what she was going to say about me. How I attempted to rape my own girlfriend. It shamed me for what I had done, to someone I cared about deeply enough to die for that person, and yet the addictive behavior of my sexual interaction drove her away. She ended the relationship by leaving me hanging out to dry at my birthday party that same year. Then she profusely insulted my person by saying I had a small penis and continuing to say I was an asshole. I could agree with her on the second part. I felt like one too.

I later found out that my best friend, the giant ogre of a goliath, whom I saved in my first grade year, was being asked out by her while we were still dating. I don't know if it was true or not. I think that he was lying to make me feel better. But it made my aggression towards her worse than before. How could she hit on my best friend while she was dating me? I was her man and she was my woman.

Later I found out that she was dating a jock. Not much of a jock. He was the benchwarmer that was beat up by my ape of a friend. She was the one who threw him against a locker and told the jock that she was his God now! It was sweet revenge at its finest hour.

My ex-girlfriend told me later that she was sorry for breaking it off with me for the stupid jockstrap. He was a bigger whinny baby than even I was. We both laughed, but I never got to see much of her after that year. I spotted her in the hallways of the high school, and she would insult my manhood even still. But I still cared for her even though I seemed to not care at all.

I don't understand why a man and an ape of a woman can't be friends and only friends. We were a pair of misfit teens in high school. She was loud and obnoxious, and I was the one with the perverted mindset that set her off on laughter. We would be joking about various things and we even made teachers come out of their rooms we would be laughing so hard at the jokes we all told each other. Little did this ape of a friend know that I was trying to use her to get to a short, hot, blond, girl with big gifts that only God could give to her?

She had the voice of a chipmunk, but she was a good singer, and I attempted for years to try and be with her, but again another failure, and another crush on me from a fat relative of hers. It seemed all that I could attract were fat women, blond fat women, big breasted blond fat women, and they all looked similar to my cousin, who raped me. It seemed for the longest time all of the girls that liked me resembled my cousin's physique. Back then I cared how women looked next to me. I was idealistic in my ways. I hated myself for it afterwards, because it didn't allow me to meet people the way I wanted to. I hurt someone, who didn't deserver to be hurt, by my words or actions.

I dated a girl over the phone only and when I actually saw a picture of her I felt ashamed to call her my girlfriend, and I dumped her for the other girl who was less ugly in my own eyes.

God had his own way to punish me for the rude awakening that I gave that girl. The one girl I was after, the hot, short, blond girl in most of my classes, was about to get married, right before I asked her to be my girlfriend. She was only fifteen years old at the time. I was shocked and stunned by the action. She didn't even have a boyfriend a week or two ago, but then she was getting married? It was for real. She wasn't pulling any punches on me. She got married and moved with her newfound husband down to Texas or California; whichever one has the huge naval base. In any case I never saw her again either.

In this big scheme of things that God had planned out for me, I felt like I was just not going anywhere with my life the way it was. Everyone, and everything I came into contact with rejected me. I felt like a fly that a frog would catch and then spit out because it wasn't good enough to swallow or even taste. The next girl, another blond, a little on the heavy side, but she would have moved away the week I had asked her out. She moved to Chicago. God, once again, intervened with his fate. I couldn't get a date if I told the girl I was dying. Believe me I tried, it didn't work.

At this point of trying to feel accepted by people, I moved on to other avenues of relationships. I could keep friendships, but I couldn't keep girlfriends. So I tried to work for a living and make my own money to impress the ladies.

I earned money as a carhop at an A & W restaurant. There I bussed tables, served food and beverages, broke mugs, and car windows. I think that must have been in the job description, because I never got fired and I was always getting great tips from the people. Either that or they felt sorry for me, and how hard I worked to please those people.

I could come home from being a carhop with as little as five dollars to as much as two hundred or three hundred dollars in one night during the fair time. It was an extremely fun place to work, but it wasn't for me to keep working there forever. I wanted to do more with my life. I wanted to have just about every waitress in the place. I tried again I failed miserably.

I again met up with a blond haired, big breasted, girl, but this time with a skinny body. She was pregnant, and in love with another man, but that didn't stop her from flirting to the point of erection. For me it was business as usual until she allowed me to feel her up constantly and she seemed to like it as well. She would allow me to watch her in the bathroom, or sneak a peak at her breasts, not at her nipples though. Those were off limits.

At work, the team was great to me. They were another extended family of sorts. They were all friendly, and they enjoyed being there for me when I needed them. The money I had earned throughout the week meant I could now buy nice clothes, and videogames for myself instead of my parents buying me clothes for once. They always wondered why I hated wearing the clothes that they picked out for me. Well, it was because they were all for littler children with bigger sizes of bellies. Yeah, I am talking like Big Bird shirts, briefs instead of boxer shorts, and the thick pop-bottle glasses instead of thin frames and tinted lenses.

Towards the end of the school year, I didn't have money, a girlfriend, or even a ride outside of having my parents take me places, or riding my bike to places. I was still alone, still ashamed, and I was still with out someone to show me affection and love. I had love all around me, but I wasn't in love with a person, not yet!

While I found having sexual intercourse with my cousins to be a relieving aspect of my tenth grade year, I hated the idea that I was having sexual relationships with people who said that they cared about me in a different way and they then proceeded to screw me while I was asleep in bed. But I was about to get even with them for that pain. The pain my female cousin had pushed onto me.

The night of our final show at the high school, I went over to my aunt and uncle's house to prepare and get ready for the show. I slipped downstairs quietly, and I snuck into the bedroom of my cousin. I then waited until she was bent over and I lifted her skirt and grabbed her throat, forcing her down over the bed. I pulled down her panties, and I proceeded to rape her back just as bad as she raped me so many times. It felt good to get even with her for that.

After I finished inside of her, I pushed her down into the bed and told her to get upstairs and to get going to the final show. At that show she was so red in her face that she almost couldn't play her trumpet. It was there that I was satisfied with getting even with her for what she had done to me. After that I never did any sort of sexual act with her again. It was like she understood that I was fed up with the game, and I wanted to be left alone in that way. I told them all that I wanted to be left out of their games, and I wanted to have a real girlfriend, and no one was going to hurt me any more.

It was shortly after this that our whole family started to fall apart. My father was attempting to reconcile with his father. To no avail, they were still butting heads until his newly remarried bride attempted to kill him and throw him out into the cold winter snow. My grandfather was a WWII veteran, with two purple hearts from two different wars. There he was a hero. In my life he was nothing but a zero. Absent in all aspects of my life, and I didn't care whether he lived or died.

My father, being the brave and generous man he was said that he was going to help him out no matter what my grandfather did to my father or me in the past. His wife was then out of the picture for a while. And I didn't want any part of my grandfather's money or anything to do with him over the years.

That summer, I spent most of my time with my ogre friend, and my younger cousin to the one I raped in previous sections of this chapter. There we were smoking marijuana, getting high, and attempting to cause trouble. Both of them helped me to get girls, but the ogre of a friend helped me to still a girlfriend from another friend of mine, who later turned out to be a gay menace of a person. The ogre friend helped me find my future wife.

That same summer, along with meeting my future wife, I found myself being friends with potential benefits, with other girls. Another heavy, blond girl that was always infatuated with me and a Hispanic girl that was so into just making men scream in a jealous rage for more.

The heavy girl and the Latino girl were both friends of sorts, but both were also very much in each other's faces and sleeping with each other's boyfriends. Each one would have the other one check out their boy toys before they would date them. Their method of ruining men was, a kind of faithfulness check-in, to see if he was going to cheat on the girl.

With my morality counter, I would put myself at null and zero. I tried to hit on anything that moved at my direction that year. I never had sex with them, but I really wanted to. So much that I about took all of the Latino girls clothes off of her before she walked through the door.

Another issue just after I met with my future wife was with the girl I almost slept with the year before. She had invited my Italian friend and myself over to play strip poker with her and another friend.

During the game we were letting the girls win a few and lose a few, but then we went full throttle with them. We took off all of their clothes and made them pay back dearly for not allowing us to see before hand. My nerdy friends sister then appeared out of her room and went right by as though nothing was going on. She even attempted to join in on the event. Which I wouldn't have minded much, but she was sleeping with some strange nut job in the other room.

The other girl was yet another blond, with big breasts, skinny, and very sluttish towards me. She was playing with my penis under the table, and I was playing with her vaginal areas. When she was down to her bra coming off, I was excited and about half naked, but then the nerds friend called on the phone to come over and help figure something out about someone or something. I wasn't paying attention, but I did pay attention to her when she said that her friend would just barge in and if she saw our bodies in the disarray that they were in now she would have flipped out on us.

The girl described to you is a girl, who is trapped inside of a girl's body of a man. If she were to hit you, it left a bruise no matter how hard it was. Her soft hit was most guys' hardest hits. But everyone blamed it on her brothers beating on her when she was little. But I disagree with that I think she held her own against them.

So as we ran around with our heads cut off and our minds in a blender to find our clothes, we finally made our way to the different parts of the house where the hot blond girl and I were face to face and making out for a bit. She didn't want to sleep with me, but I wanted to feel her whole body up and down. She then asked for my class ring, but I had to tell her no unless she would sleep with me at least once, otherwise it was no deal.

That summer I called up on a lot of girls to get the high of them being with me, and then once I was done I would just hang up the phone and tell them I loved them. Even though I didn't really know what I was saying to them about love, that is.

My curse for some reason didn't work on the phone. I could talk women into doing anything over long distances, but get them up next to me, forget it. They would see something in me that was either scary or innocent that they didn't want to damage or ruin. God put something in my eyes to reflect their true feelings towards me, and it left me with a single person, who I know now that I love dearly, but at the time I was in it to win the sex and the girl from my other friend again who was later found out to be gay.

The Latino girl and I grew closer as friends. I think that she was the first girl that I never wanted to have sex with after that short spurt of intimacy on my parents couch. I got a great review back though from her. The one thing that I can really say that was good about this Latino girl was that she helped me to overcome my fear of prejudice in people.

She took me to an area in her neighborhood that was rundown, beat up, and in massive need of renovations on every building. To her this was her neighborhood and her family lived in these places. She told me that when she comes to my area, she feels scared because she sees people with a bias against her because of her skin color and her eyes look different. She said that she and I hadn't done anything wrong, but it is just the way some people see the world, and that is what was wrong. After that conversation I was glad to have met with her. She was so intelligent in her own right about prosperity and racism. She and I would continue this same conversation for several months, which seemed like years in the sky well of the high school.

That same summer, I was invited to a birthday party for my twin friends that were neighbors to my ogre friend. They were celebrating at "Adventureland", where the initial intent was to hook the gay friend of ours up with this hot, quiet, blond, with big breasts, and a very punctual attitude that made mine seem all the better.

As the day went on he tried to ask her out, and never drew up the courage to ask her. The two rode ride after ride, but he was too nervous. As the time drew closer to closing time at the park, he was determined to go ask her out on a date. After all the two of them had been talking for about three or four months prior to this. She seemed to be interested, in a weird way, but he didn't want to see her in the same light as she saw him I guess. So one of the twin-girls pushed me to go on a ride with her in the infamous "outlaw gulch". There we rode a spinning circle ride where this beautiful young attractive girl rode along side me and she pressed her body close to mine. I was losing my breath on the ride, and from looking into her beautiful grey eyes. It felt like I had known her my whole life in one day of meeting up with her. God had put her in my space, and the twins pushed me to ask her to be my girlfriend. We agreed we would be friends first, but for the gay man's misdirected acts of cowardice, he missed the opportunity completely that day.

I did feel bad about taking away his opportunity, but he found out later that we were a much more suited couple than anyone could have imagined.

And so we went to the theatre in the park and watched a show in the back of the theatre. There we looked at each other, held each other's hands and then I did what any good sexual addict would do. I attempted to play with her body in any sexual way that I could without being too perverse about it in front of all of those people.

After the show we all went to our designated areas of arrival and left each other in the dust. I didn't know if I was going to see that girl ever again, but I had this feeling that she was a perfect fit to my collection of imaginary women I would have sex with in the future. I didn't know that I would have had a longer relationship with her than previous girls from my past.

As you have already read, my story is one that quite possibly could have been helped in a lot of different ways, but that isn't where it ended. I kept going on with my addiction, keeping it hidden from the world until now. One thing that I wanted out of this book was to make sure you, as a reader understood the truth about sex and love addiction.

As an addict to this kind of behavior, I have a much harder time to separate my feelings from my emotions and those people who I have emotions for I sometimes will think of them as being in love with me.

Everyday people are hurt by someone like me, and I can't imagine what the victim would have to go through to get over that pain and anguish any more than what I went through, but I know that what I did was wrong to others, but when you are fighting with your own morality and existence you will do some stupid things to be in control of your own body.

At this point I hope you understand it better, and how the sexual addiction starts with abuse and sex, and then turns into more abuse. It is not some sort of a light switch that can be turned on or off. It too, a chemical imbalance of sorts, when we use our bodies to explore sex for the first time we need to understand that sex sometimes can be seen and used as a weapon of destruction, humiliation, or even torture, like in my own case with my brother.

The decease is passed down by generational gaps and is becoming a family secret across the board. In performing a search on the Internet at any point in time, you will see if you look up the word "PORN" it will come back with enough web sites to allow a single site for each person here on earth. I searched for that word and found over 6.5 billion pages dedicated to the kind of things that people say they don't want their children to watch. When it is in front of you as big as 6.5 billion pages, I would think that one or two children would be seeing it and learning about sex without guidance from a trusted adult. Keep that thought in your mind as you read the last two chapters.

Chapter 11

New Year, New York City

It is much harder to live with this problem than it is to read a book about it. Sex and love addiction are very deadly. Depending on who the other people had sex with I could have contracted a disease at any point in time. My cousins were sleeping with me along with various other people. Anyone of them might have contracted a disease from someone else spreading the virus or parasites. There are diseases that do cause death that many sexually active people carry that aren't transmitted through normal sexual contact. And they are curable if caught in time, but if they are left unattended will damage organs in your body causing you to die a horrible death. You might want to think about that the next time you have monogamous sex.

My story seems to have hit rock bottom, but it actually only started with my 10th grade year. In my junior year of high school I was about to embark into a situation where being a pervert was my role in the hallways.

All of the people in my family, including those who were having sex with me, were clueless about everyone else's role in molesting me for some reason. My father thought that I learned about sex and masturbation from when I walked in on him doing the deed on a chair when I came home from school one afternoon. He had a yeast infection from my mother who was apparently not so popping fresh.

My brother had hints that I was sleeping with my other cousins, but he didn't care because I was his puppet as well. My cousins didn't know my brother was having sex with me because I was keeping it hidden like my brother told me to. I didn't want to die by his hands? He was cruel and conceded. He would have done it too if he knew he could get away with it. But for all of those who hurt my feelings in life, I was about to become unhinged!

That year I felt rage, anger, and aggression for anyone who dared to tempt my ego. I had lustful thoughts of raping women and men. I had thoughts of killing others that would make fun of me. I could have acted on then without even breaking a sweat, but I chose to leave it alone. I cared too much about life as it was, and I was happy to be with someone who wanted to be with me. I still believe that God put her in my path to stop me from performing what I was thinking of doing to the bully jocks that were causing me grief during the school day.

My oldest cousin, loved to be forced upon, and I did that already. I was done with her, and I moved on and told her I was through. I couldn't figure out why anyone would want to be raped. I didn't think you could rape someone who was willing to have sex with you. But then again I didn't know having sex was wrong unless you were married or in a committed relationship until recently.

I would desperately make my attempts to touch women in private areas of their body causing what seemed like an accident to the untrained eye, was actually a violation of a person's virginity and tranquility in their own personal space. With how immoral and un-normal I was to be seen, I would think I would have been caught much sooner than this, but I was never spoken to about it. Not in private, or in public. People in my classes would see my feet stretch out and go up a girls skirt ever so smoothly, but to no avail, I was left only fondling the buttocks or another region of the body.

I would go home and dream even more about having sex with each of the women I touched that day. I would get arousals throughout the day and express great joy for heading home where I could relieve my aggressions and horniness on a computer screen, or a pornographic image.

The people that seemed to get in my way of satisfying my craving for rubbing up against other girls in my classes were expendable creatures. They were like ants in my ant farm. I had images in my mind of curb stomping their heads and spitting on the corpses.

In my imagination I would torture them to the point of death, and then I would sexually molest them while rigor set in. I felt like my abusive thoughts got even darker than those of my brother's thoughts. I didn't want to actually kill the people, but a part of my aggression wanted them out of my life for good. I lived to screw with other people's minds as I dreamt of hurting those people who would cause me any form of pain.

My pain was much more desperate than those you see in today's society. Even though I didn't act on them, I wanted to so badly. I was insulted my entire school life up to this point, and I was done taking crap from others in my own life. I wanted my life back, and I wasn't going to let anyone hurt me more. I had sticks and stones thrown at me, and even those didn't hurt as bad as the words that were being said about me. People, who knew me and those who didn't want to know me, said the words. It was hard to live a life in the dark of night just to make it through the day.

That year, though I was being humiliated, the women could tell something different about me. They could tell something about how I might have had a girlfriend that year. I was getting more and more attention from other women. It was almost as though women know when a man is single and when the man is seeing someone.

At first I thought the word got out that I was seeing this girl from a rival school, but no one had even mentioned it. How was it that, I was driving these women off of my back, to the point of hurting myself? My girlfriend wasn't there with me. She wasn't even known by anyone at the school. How then did her presence become known to everyone around me?

Girls would walk up to me and say hello! They would go by and give me hugs bigger than I would do to most people. And the second I turned single for a week, the girls all said I was sexually harassing them. And yes we did break our relationship off for a week after I found out she was wearing some dumb jock's letterman jacket.

I made the mistake of thinking that she was actually dating this other jock. I then proceeded to check out my other options, namely one of my ex-girlfriends, who were giving out sexual favors like candy. I spoke to her over the phone and attempted to have phone sex with her. She agreed, but then realized I was using her and telling her that I had broken it off with my, what was now my ex-girlfriend, and that she was the only one for me. This of course was a lie to get her to talk dirty and potentially come over to my house?

The next morning I was called into the principal's office, sat down next to her, and then I was told that I had sexually harassed her. I didn't think that it was when she was cooperative about the whole thing, but when I hung up after getting off the bus, I guess that she didn't like that feeling and so she turned me in for sexual harassment.

After that day, somehow my ex-girlfriend had changed her mind and decided to stay with me. She called me back and explained that she thought that I cheated on her with one of my ex-girlfriends; I explained my situation and told her that I was not with her at the time, and that she was the one who got me into trouble, and tried to not allow us to get back together.

In making-up, we decided it was time to meet her parents. Then for the first time I met someone who was slimier and more sinister than I was at my own game. Her father was very devilish in all of his tactics. Sleeping around with other women was his specialty. He was also an alcoholic with a very bad temper for violence.

He beat his own wife while my girlfriend was still in the womb of her real mother. He of course did similar things with his new wife as well, but she wasn't quite as dramatic about the whole thing, and decided to stay around for more punishment. I think that she found out how much money he was worth and stuck with it.

I still wanted to be with that girl from my first year in high school. While I had a girlfriend at another high school, I hung out with the Latino girl in the halls rather than continuing my efforts too much more with my beautiful brown haired priceless work of art. She was still seeing jerks for boyfriends. Then I met my first drug-dealing friend in high school.

He was a smart mouthed punk kid that always made fun of those who didn't smoke weed with him. He sat in the stairwells of the school with his gay friend and belittled and rate girls as they went past. Both of them were almost too close to being straight. They rated women on a scale of 1 to 10.

They waited for a girl to pass by only to belittle them behind their backs. They would enter the women's restroom and then the judging began. Of course, in their book no one was as beautiful or worthy of a 10 except for the pop singer "Mariah Carey".

To those two boys in suede, she was their top-notch class of woman. Of course every other model or dog of a girl was nowhere even close to her perfect body and voice. All other women to them were nothing.

I, on the hand, not to break down Mariah, thought that the two boys were being rude and conceded. They treated women with a huge lack of respect and they had a very disfigured look at what women were supposed to be like. Not that I did, I just used them as objects. And yes that was a joke to bash my old self.

I wasn't going to stand around the two and be sought after for sexual harassment again. So I continued my days hanging out with either my brunette friend from my first day of choir, or I would hang out with my Latino friend in the upper north sky walk area. The game for those two men was just that, a game. But for me it was much more than a game, it was my lives work being played out in a horrible onslaught of mockery towards women's breasts, butts, or other areas of hygiene.

For me it was something that seemed so real for the longest time, but rather than confront the issues before me I left them behind like the cowardice person I was back then. The way that those two judged those women was almost the same way the world treated me and judged me on a daily basis. I was nothing more than a number to the world. I felt like I was a zero on a scale of 1 to 10.

I keep seeing a pattern of men and women treating each other with very little respect or graceful applause. I was treating my girlfriend in this way anytime I saw her. In my mind it was as though I was mistreating her by being a gentleman for her. Even she refused to allow me to open doors for her after a while, which made me think that she didn't want to be treated in that way.

All of the actions that kept taking place were crowding around my mind. The words were closing in and causing me so much pain and agony. I knew for some reason, I didn't want to be treated that way. I always wanted to be treated special with the woman I loved.

I attempted so many stupid moves after I heard those words come out of her mouth. She wanted me to stop opening the doors for her, and being polite in front of her. She wanted me to make her equal to herself. I was not about to insult her any further. So I stopped with the romance, with the flowers, and with the notes. I didn't know what to do or say around her or any other girl for that matter. Why did I get the idea that women loved jerks for men? Everywhere I went, everywhere I turned a corner, and men and women were constantly treating each other like slaves. I was being treated like a slave in my own life until then. Was I the person in the wrong for caring for another person and not treating them like they were nothing? Had all of the movies lied about chivalry?

I felt like I was the jerk for being a nice person to everyone I came in contact with. I attempted to open doors for women including my girlfriend only to have them rip the door right out of my hand and tell me to get going as if I were to do some sort of damage if they were to go in first. I was getting tired of this whole being kind to women sort of thing and the romance I felt was pure good to do was out, and I felt like my relationship with my girlfriend was right along with it. That's when I attempted to cheat on my girlfriend with just about every girl in high school.

I felt like I needed sex to calm my nerves down. It was a craving that I had to have more than air. The people would think that I was crazy looking at all of the women with one thing in mind. Sex! I would be hunched over looking down at the ground, but as soon as an attractive person walked by I had an eye up looking to see up a dress or down their shirts to catch a glimpse of a breast.

I attempted to start getting in good with girls of my friends. I worked hard at making everyone else look bad so that I could get the girls. I went to my friends' girlfriends' homes and make passes at them with no success at all. It almost became a pattern of bad behaviors after the next one, but yet I was criticizing others for similar tactics of flailing with other women. People would tell my girlfriend that she needed to break it off with me because I was cheating on her. I didn't look at it as cheating because I didn't get anywhere with any of them. They all dumped me out the door as I lay drooling over their hot bodies.

Either the girl would get scared and run, or they would know my girlfriend, and not want to hurt her feelings. At least that was what was told to me.

Every time I attempted to perform the act of cheating, I felt even more miserable than the time before. When I went to school the next day, I stayed away from the person whom I attempted to have my way with. I would bargain with them asking them to not tell another person about the problems I caused the night before.

I many times stopped myself short of them all except for one girl who I took to the room where I was raped and I had her give me an oral massage. Shortly after that she was grounded, because she wrote about it to a friend that she was going to have sex with me some time. She didn't care that I was dating someone else, of course neither did I. It was sex, and I only cared about the sex. It was becoming my drug of choice.

The phrase "It's a small world!" isn't just a song. It is the punch line to the jokes about my life. I thought that I would have been done for since she told her friends what she had done. Many of the people that knew the girl I had done this with were also friends to many people who knew I was dating my girlfriend at the time.

Shortly after that brief spurt of womanizing, I found myself being hit on by girl after girl. My girlfriend and I went to her homecoming that same year. While we were there I was asked to slow dance with a much more attractive looking girl than my girlfriend was, or so I thought at the time. So I asked my girlfriend if it was all right since this other girl went stag. She quickly said it was fine with her and I left to the dance floor of the Historical Center. Then a switch happened in the middle of the dance when the girl's friend wanted to dance with me and practically have sex on the floor. I quickly stopped and looked at my girlfriend, and refused to dance anymore. I saw tears running down her eyes as she was crying like I was enjoying the company of the other girls, but I was only trying to help others, but she didn't see it in that way at first. I then asked her if we could leave and I would go home with her if she wanted me to.

We quickly removed ourselves from the party and went out for a walk to her car. She was so upset that I thought that I would never get to see her beautiful eyes ever again. I then told her exactly what had happened and the reason I ended up with the other girl was because they pulled a switch on me and I didn't even want to dance with her. I then apologized to her and we drove home.

In the driveway we sat in the car with the windows down. We looked out at the stars and listened as nothing happened around us. We turned off the lights and we made out for the first time. But I waited for her to make the next move of sex. I didn't get sex that night, but I was so close. That was what was going on in my head.

That year for our annual trip with the choir, we took off to St. Louis again for a second time. I somehow managed to keep my composure for most of the trip. But after about five minutes into driving down to Missouri, I found that no one was next to me to keep me company on the trip. Moving forward, away from being alone that is to say, my feelings for others slowly dwindled to nothing more than a stone cold hard without feeling.

We went down to the heritage festival for choirs in the Midwest region, and we took second place out of two that year. We went to the ceremony and received the second place trophy. I thought it wasn't too bad, but not to good either, seeing how we came in second out of two groups. Then it was time to party after the ceremony.

I again was left alone at the dance floor. No one would dance with me the entire time we were there. I attempted to not think about my role in the choir for a while and then I decided to call home and talk with my girlfriend. She was fine, but she was also grounded from watching television, because of the way she did the dishes or something.

I then told my girlfriend goodbye and that I loved her very much. I then went back to the party where I met a girl from Texas who was very flirtatious with me. She did this until I told her I was just getting off of the phone with my girlfriend. Then she ran and hid until I was out of sight.

Later I found out that this girl was the choir director's daughter from the Texas group that was there. The girl wanted to take me back to her room and bump the ugly train. Talk about my good behavior. I was so angry at my own words that I couldn't do anything except cry. I totally blew any chance of even being a friend to her. Then I remembered that I was committed to my girlfriend back in Iowa.

I stepped back out to the party after I regained my composure from the crying I did. I looked at everyone else dancing around me. I was alone and so I sat at the corner and waited for my dance with my brown haired friend from my freshman year yet again telling me I would have a dance with her, only to get rejected for all three years of competitions. This was my final year to have had at least one dance with my friend, and show her that I had some rhythm in my soul for her.

The next thing I knew we were on our way back home to Iowa. What happened to the dancing, well it must have left without me, because I didn't get to see it at all. One thing that I could never understand is that women say that they hate men who are jerks, but then they date, and even marry them in the end.

When we got home from Missouri, our choir director brought seven of the students into her office, including myself. She had a surprise come in the mail about an opportunity to sing at the Carnegie Hall in New York City.

Our teacher had a Jazz musician, sister that lived in the city, and so our teacher wanted take us there for a concert, a Broadway play, and a night out on the town in New York City. We all worked hard to get there too!

Fundraisers, pie sales, carwashes, and various other activities to gain money to go, we didn't have a clue it would have cost us so much, but we ended up not having to pay for anything out of pocket, when we went. We had money for souvenirs, but that was about it. I was wondering why certain people were able to go, but my brunette friend of the first year wasn't able to go.

She was every bit as capable of a singer as I was, or anyone else on that roster of students. But she had to keep it a secret, and she didn't want everyone to go. And so our teacher only picked a select few. All of the students were snooty kids with very involved parents. I hated almost all of the people I went with that summer, but we eventually made a bond as we sang in the streets of New York City.

While in New York City I continued to think with the wrong head, and I kept causing trouble for myself, but I didn't care. I was in another world full of life and people dying to get into a Broadway Musical. I wanted to be part of the action in all of them, but I was not fit for the roles, not yet anyway.

The closet gay boy, who loved Mariah, was constantly taking us on a trip to see a place where she had performed in New York City in years past. One time in the entire trip we actually saw her driving her SUV down a main roadway in the center of Manhattan.

We took tours of St. Paul's Cathedral, the Empire State building, The Statue of Liberty was closed, we went to the Today Show, we sat and ate at an Italian restaurant where our teacher's sister worked as a Jazz musician, and we closed down a Karaoke bar. Finally, we ended the tour with a visit to the Broadway musical Les Miserable. It was a special performance of the British cast from England. The places we saw were inspiring to say the least.

We made quick tours of Central Park on a horse drawn carriage. We stepped in and out of the Ritz Carlton hotel, and we all went shopping at Macy's. The city was a living and moving machine. Everything moved at a fluid pace, and if you didn't you were road pizza.

Everyday, we would meet the director of the choir that we were about to sing with. Renee Clausen. He would tell us about times when people would say that they knew him, but refer to his name as a woman's name as he stood near the men as they spoke about his music referring to him as a woman. He then went over and signed his autograph on the sheet music in front of the two men speaking, and walked away.

He had the entire choir of over 300 people working for nearly eight hours a day to prepare for the end of the week's show. We worked on every detail down to the finest of notes, punctuation, and staccato increments of each note.

The final day came where we would have to practice for three hours in the Carnegie Hall. Once inside you could tell it was a much bigger place than it looked. Outside it looked like an old firehouse of sorts. Inside it looked like an Opera house with all of the trimmings attached, and it sounded like an acoustic paradise.

As we practiced it was like an angelic sound surrounded us and we were not even singing the songs. The sound couldn't penetrate the walls and bounced back at the stage causing an echoing effect that would bring anyone to their knees if they heard it. Finished our practice runs in the hall, and we felt ready for the night. We then parted ways to go after some food for our empty stomachs.

After lunch, we all gathered together to practice getting on the stage and off of the stage. While we were waiting in line outside of the hall, we were greeted by a bag lady with a garbage bag dress. It was almost like a dress you would see in a shopping center except it had the word glad written all over it, and it was almost see through to the point of noticing every body part when the light from the sun hit the dress at certain angles. The bag lady herself, looked like a zombie in her movement and actions. She must have been drinking to be moving the way that she was and with the figure of a body she had he didn't eat much either. It made me feel saddened to see such a place with beauty on the inside and refugees on the outside. It was truly in my mind what I pictured Jesus to look like now.

A man behind me stood in the same line, and preceded to instruct several other people to become part of his new game of bravery and wits, he called it the penis game. I asked the man what the penis game was being curiously stupid in my youth. I found out that you can say penis in just about any wording of a song and never hear the person singing it unless it was a solo. To me it seemed like a challenge and very interesting at the same time. The object of the penis game was to say penis the loudest and not get caught during the music.

At the end of each song, a flood of applause would come crashing back at the stage creating a tidal wave of sound crashing back into all of the singers. The show seemed to go flawlessly. We were applauded for what seemed like hours after. Then we left to fill our stomachs from the exhausting performance we endured.

We headed out on the town for one last fling. We ate at our teacher's sister's restaurant and listened to her sister sing. Our teacher also sang that night, at a Karaoke bar in Queens. We had a fun time that night. I didn't want it to end.

The whole time I was there in New York City, I felt alone. The people were rude, my cohorts' were ignoring my every word, and I was copping a feel like I was waiting for the end of the world to come that day.

Coming home from New York City, I could see the nasty look on their faces as I ran to my family. Their look of disgust and shame for me were very noticeable. I on the other end felt like I was a monster that was untouchable by anyone, unloved by my own family and friends, and left out in the cold to fend for my own way of life as I knew it.

The monster I am speaking of would cause pictures to appear in my mind about how I needed to rape each one of them choosing to allow me to suffer horrifyingly. I was desperate in all of my attempts at getting the attention I needed during every trip I had ever taken, but the sexual urges kept me from being close to anyone because I was always afraid of what I would do to have the sex even more than the friendships.

I kept feeling like everyone else had something that I never had. Virginity was something I was lacking in my life. I wanted a life without sexual thoughts, and a way to show real love for another human being. The problem was that I was never really shown love from the humans that took care of me, or at least I didn't know what that love was.

As I got home from the trip, I quickly unpacked and began scanning through the pornography that I had collected from my father's stash. I didn't care how disgusting the pages seemed to be, I was looking at the women.

In my mind I mutilated each girl as I imagined each student who went on that trip with me to New York City. I put the heads of the girls over the years on the bodies of the super models in the magazines, and I hurt them just like they hurt me.

The next day I received my certificate to get my Driver's license from the D.O.T. There I looked at my old permit to drive, and I saw that I still had my high school baseball hat on in the picture. I wasn't aware until then that my hat was on in that picture. The clerk at the counter said it was illegal to have my ID with my hat on like that. I asked if I could keep it, but then the clerk shredded it right in front of me. But I did get my first driver's license that day. And I couldn't wait to try out my aunt's old vet. Chevette that is!

It was a car that was economical in its own means. It was dark-blue, sparkled paint, almost no rust spots, very compact, and very beat up from years of wear and tear.

My girlfriend and I drew very close in that car. In fact you had to be very close in that car; it was so small that my giant friend couldn't even get in without rolling up into a ball, with his knees against his chest. But it never did break down on me. It had an oil leak that I caused from all of the speeding I did when I was with my girlfriend.

One evening on our way home from a movie, she asked me in that car if I loved her. I told her I did, but the truth was that I didn't even know what love was for me. I guess I answered her right because I had sex with her in the front seat outside of her father's house.

The next morning I felt like I was going to be sick. Something came onto me like a hot sun. I then decided to go to school any way. I remembered the night before and how scared I was that she was possibly pregnant. I couldn't believe I didn't want to wait longer, but then again it was nice to have a relationship go further this time. I think part of the way life goes is dependent on God's will for us, and I believe that God puts us where we need to be when we need him the most.

I was at school that morning. The news was on, and we were all watching as a burgundy vehicle was getting the Jaws-of-life attached to it. I didn't think anything of it at first. It was by my girlfriend's school, and I had prayed that God wouldn't allow her to be pregnant that night before the accident. God answered my prayers I guess.

She was traveling to school that morning. She was in a hurry to get there after making a pit stop at a breakfast place near the school. She had problems with seizures in the past, but this same problem also made her left side blind at a certain angle. The truck that hit her was in that angle of view, and she left the intersection and got hit at 35 mph.

She was sent across her front seat to the passenger's side where she stopped, but the car kept rolling. Her shoes stayed in place on the pedals. Her clothing was bloody from the glass and the impact of the truck hitting her. She ended up with several broken bones, a fractured collar bone, and various other injuries. She was very glad she didn't wear her seatbelt that day because if she had the truck would have killed her by the impact and not being able to move away from the force.

My first thought was that she was dead as I watched on the news. The accident was shown on television, and I saw the truck still in the side of the car on the driver's side. I thought for sure she was pinned inside and bleeding out. I also thought that she may be pregnant as well. Oh, great! What a way to find out she was pregnant. With her whole family gathered around her and in a comatose state. Her father had previously caught us making out in the basement of his house, which was something I couldn't really deal with, and if I had to add the idea of her being pregnant, it wouldn't have been much more fun than the last time.

She was broken, beat up, battered, and bruised, but not totally out of commission. She had courage, strength, and a brutal resource of power. It seemed like God had saved her from that wreckage to be my guide throughout our life together. It was though she was healed without any problems within weeks of her accident.

Her car was spread over the highway in sections. As I looked at the wreckage, I stood with a huge sigh of relief, both that she wasn't pregnant, and that she was still alive. I had truly come to love her or at least what I knew as being in love with her.

Later she would have come out of her wreck with nearly no problems, but I had the problem still of her father. He was not pleased that I was spending so much time with her alone, and he had a feeling like I wasn't having any kind of picnic with her. We were definitely still having sex behind closed doors even after her injuries.

One thing to bring this chapter to a close is that when a sexual addict wants sex, he or she will get it no matter how they have to get it. It is much worse than drugs or alcohol addictions because of the ease of access to pornography, prostitution rings, and various other alternatives to regulated mediums. Most of the sex addict's functions and favorites are free somewhere on the Internet, with a significant other, or with a total stranger who is also an addict of sex.

Chapter 12

My Senior Year

When I tell people my story of how I was abused they feel sorry for my inner-child. When I tell them it was from my brother and my cousins they are even more shocked, but when I tell them I continued the tradition of the rape and molesting, all gloves are off. People would almost get a violent rage to hurt me again, but that isn't what this book is about. It is about abuse endured by all sex and love addicts. It is a story of my own life, and how I treated the world that treated me badly first. For a long time I didn't believe there was a God of sorts, but I didn't know that there was freewill in my actions either.

People could change their minds if they really want the change. It took me a long time to figure this out. My addiction, and my compulsive thinking grew very strong my senior year. But God wasn't done with my freewill yet. God wanted to see me become broken inside and out. And

Satan was on the verge of seeing God's plan out for the rest of the world to see and hear. I called it my curse of the soul seen in my eyes.

The first thing that I remember about my senior year was the way I treated everyone equally. I didn't care if they were black, white, mixed, matched, or from a completely different planet. I would accept all of the people around me as my friends. And that year my table grew to a huge number of about seventy or eighty students with rotations every half hour for students with different lunch times for crowding. I had a large part of our school sitting with us during lunch, in the halls after lunch, and in the choir room for most periods. It seemed as though everyone was around me or at least near me. Of course people wanted to be near the young man with his picture on the wall standing below the Carnegie Hall in New York City. I thought that I was the stuff and the stuff that it was made from.

My senior year in high school was probably my most rewarding year in school. I had trophies, awards, and a ton of friends who loved to be around me. And although I lost one of my best friends, due to her graduating the year before I would, I handled the transition slightly better than I thought. I cried like a baby over the most beautiful creature on the planet in my own world at the time.

As I gazed at the pictures of years past in choir, and yearbooks that filled my school days, I looked back and realized I was going to miss it all, except for the parts of the books where the women wrote their phone numbers to make it a point to call me a perverted crazy young man, and to never change. That phrase was my favorite one.

One thing that we all had at our lunchroom table was love for one another. I had love for most of the women in the largest group of people I had encountered in years. We were a family of misfits and rejects larger than life and showing it proudly. No one dared mess with my group because we out numbered even the jock tables. It became a fellowship of sorts. We didn't care about our past or future, but we accepted everyone as an equal part of the larger group.

That year was a little more troublesome with my addiction. I was getting braver, and there were freshmen to hit on that didn't know who I was. And I hit on them very well that year. My mind was focused on the here and now. The freshmen girls were here and now and my girlfriend was away at a different school in a different zip code. With her out of my mind, the sexual fantasies would take over my day, and I would continue to daydream a way to sleep with every girl in my expanding group of people.

I was a sexual addict at this point. To tell if a person was a sexual addict, you would have to look at several factors of their life. That there was nothing to think about other than sex, lustful thoughts constantly, and always being the one in control of other people's wills to do things by making decisions for them.

For me sex was the same thing as loving someone, and loving someone meant you needed to have sex with them. I didn't know how to separate the two terms. When something caught my eye that I wanted to have sex with it must have meant that I loved it. If someone or something I loved walked by I wanted to sex it up a bit. I had fantasies about my friends, family, pets, and total strangers. Not that I actually had sex with any of them, but I felt like I wanted to have sex at that moment. Many times I would find ways to try and touch them inappropriately just to ease my aggression to want to do more than that.

This problem seemed to linger after my brother had left the picture, and it continued to get worse with my cousins gone away from the high school. Even with all of the people I had around me, I felt truly alone in the school without my freshman year, brunette friend from choir who graduated the previous year. Without even her to talk to about my problems I felt out of my element and all by myself. And with no one to help me release my emotions with, or no one to cry on, I had feelings of acting on the thoughts that kept running in my head.

I masturbated at least ten times per day. I would make sexual passes at girls even when my girlfriend was around me. I would go to the movies and get my penis played with while I played with my girlfriend's parts and the neighboring woman, who might have been a total stranger. My head was continuing to be filled with more and more fantasy.

That year my heart turned so cold that I had no more feeling left for caring of others. Risk of being caught didn't matter, in fact the risk made my life that much more exciting and out-of-control. I would attempt to get girls to go home with me and rape them, but my eyes would see the fear in their eyes, and I would stop and let them go. If that wasn't the case, they would figure me out far before getting into that position and run away from the danger I would be putting them into. In any case I was always unsuccessful in the attempt. Part of my mind would stop my actions from being harmful, and the other part scurrying away like a lost soul.

I had allowed the monster that was within my brother to enter into my mind and take over my spirit. The addict lied very well while inside of me. I could lie to a con artist, and it would have seemed believable. I made excuse after excuse for whatever actions I took that were bad and then I would proceed to continue them even though I didn't want to in my heart. With each lie I told I left God's will behind me and I fell down a darker and much more dangerous path.

I felt my addiction taking over my life, but it felt good to have something that I could control versus listening to

God's will over me. In that personal will, my mind slowed down to a crawl and I focused on nothing else but women, and having sexual intercourse with all of them. I am grateful that I was never successful, but I was very damaging in my attempts.

I lived in the choir room where my second family helped to feed my addictive behaviors. In the soundproof room where we would all take turns practicing, I would vent my rage out by screaming at the top of my lungs. Crying out, "Why am I doing this? Why?" only to hear dead silence. My senior year consisted of two classes, twelfth grade English and Choir. Both were my own choices, but I loved English, and I loved choir even more.

I still worked that year at the restaurant, and I still had my beast of a little car. I drove everywhere including to school, and to various malls. The malls were hotspots that caused me to spend my money from tips that the customers had left me. I would buy clothes, food, and attempt to buy the ladies.

My family at home never saw me much that year. If I wasn't sleeping in my bed, I was out with friends, on a trip to a city with the choir, at a dance, or a part of a senior function that took most of my time.

When I was home I locked myself in my room and refused to come out. Inside the room I would masturbate to pornography that I had stolen from my parents dresser drawers, or watch the pornographic videos that I found upstairs that my father used to watch while he masturbated. If I wasn't masturbating in my room, I was talking on the telephone to all of the women I had met up with on trips, or I would be talking to my girlfriend who I was still seeing.

In my junior year I had a problem with not being able to see my girlfriend, but in my senior year I had a problem with seeing her too much. It wasn't because of her, but rather her father that caused her to want to get out and see the world more for what it was instead of what her father had made it out to be like.

Her father would move around the house, trying to look like he was a cool father figure, drinking beer, smoking like a chimney, and asking stupid questions about if we wanted to drink a beer along with him or have a smoke outside with him. None of it impressed my intellect. To me he was nothing more than a grungy looking fool of a fifty-plus year old man who wanted to be a kid again. He was the type of person who didn't want anything to do with being good, but he wanted all the attention on him and him alone. He was the true addictive personality and control freak. I don't think that he could have had a good time without it.

Like her father's beer, I was being drawn into a world of addiction to sex, masturbation, and pornography. Those items ruled my time, my mind, and my life. Days were consumed by my addiction to pornography. I was getting high off of pleasing myself and ejaculating to remove the stress of my day.

I made attempts at stopping only to find out that I didn't have control over my sexual behaviors anymore than I had control over a remote without batteries inside. My heart was so cold to the outside world that I stayed in my room and did nothing but isolate myself further.

I became a puppet of my own design. I looked to others for all of the answers, and then I mimicked their answers to the letter in hopes of getting the same response. I cheated at studies in my prior years, but in my senior year I didn't have to work hard at all. I only had the choir courses and English courses. But the thing that made me the most intrigued was the fact that since I was mimicking everyone else this way, I was starting to become a popular student. I even started being liked by those who rejected me in previous years.

I grew in my popularity and I grew in my addiction. I grew mostly in my actions to take over control of my life in a negative way. I could see girls all looking to me as a sexual object, waiting to be pounced on. This was all of course being displayed in my own mind by the addiction, but I didn't care about that, I was being pleased in some fashion. I constantly had fantasies about other girls at my school. The girls who had previously been in my life and many more that were still going to school at my high school were causing me a lot of grief and pain as I attempted to ask them out to dances.

My senior year, I was threatened by my friends to not go any further with the girls at my high school because it would have hurt my girlfriends love for me. I was so caught up in the excitement though that I couldn't stop then even with the outcome being that drastic. I, instead of telling my friends whom I was trying to score with, decided to keep it all a secret and leave the telling to my own mind. Each time I drew closer to a girl in my school I attempted to stop myself, but every effort was without success. I couldn't stop myself from viewing the pornographic movies, looking at the magazines, or trying to bring home a girl a night. I did it in my mind. No girls actually wanted me, and I didn't want them if the rejected me. I raped them in my mind to the point of killing them. They stole my heart in my mind and I was going to replace it with theirs. My thoughts of fantasy started to become more like reality, and as I looked people in the face of being turned in to authorities, the person usually turned tail and ran as they saw the redness in my eyes explode with anger.

When I could find a girl to take somewhere, I could see the scared look and feelings in their eyes. My mind was saying keep going she is only scared because it's her first time. I would start and stop almost instantly of each other voice that mounted inside of my head.

As I ran into my girlfriend's father more and more, I was constantly being aggravated by his actions of rage towards my character. He would continue to belittle me like my brother did. It made me want to kill him. He made my heart beat so fast that the adrenalin was rushing to my head just enough to get the energy to leave. I knew in my own mind it wasn't worth the effort to hurt him, and I would probably go to jail.

I could tell that what he said to her about me was also hurting her heart. He would tell her that I as a no-good son of a bitch, and she deserved better than that. He would attempt to get me to leave her by telling me objectifying details about her hygiene like: "She doesn't take baths" or "She doesn't brush her teeth." It didn't matter to me obviously I was still with her. He didn't understand my problems, or me and I believe that by my standing up to his person, it made me want to be there all the more, if only to piss him off. My girlfriend was beautiful and very kind to me. There was no way I was going to give her up for anyone, not even her father.

I could see how they were whispering to one another about how this was her first and only boyfriend. I thought to myself, "How could her own family be so cruel to mention that while she was right in front of them?" It had to hurt her feelings, because it hurt me just to listen in on the conversation. Then it dawned on me that their thoughts of my girlfriend, and their niece, were as messed up as my family had been with my life.

After that experience we became inseparable and we lived on each other's thoughts of marriage and love. But the problem I had with marriage was that it was so permanent, and in my mind I wanted things to continue to happen with other people in my life. I wasn't ready to settle down, I had too many skeletons in my closet.

While we were still dating, my girlfriend thought of me as a loyal person who loved others with the same compassion as I did her. She definitely gained my attention, as I grew closer to her and her body. I itemized everyone I looked upon for sexual bliss. Even the ones who were being looked at had their clothes stripped from them in my mind.

My brother on the other hand continued his torture of my step-nephew from my brother's wife's first marriage. My brother would constantly be worried about my actions and voice as I grew up. He was constantly bothered by the idea that I would tell people about the abuse I endured from the time I was five until the age of about fifteen. I ruled the day my brother awaited for, when I would confess my problems of abusing me sexually, it finally had come, but that was much later than these events.

Graduation came much before that date. It came quicker than I thought it could possibly come. I felt like there were thousands of people cheering for me when I walked the stage. Students in the graduation choir raised their voices to shout out my name. It was in that group that I was loved by nearly all of the students, but outside I was considered an outcast. But why might you ask was a crowd of people cheering for me.

That year my giant of a friend and I, mostly due to the quite nature of our beings, and our attempts to allow anyone and everyone sit with us in a huge display of affection during lunch, demonstrated that love over popularity ruled our school that year. We had close to eighty students attended lunch at the same time all sitting around table. The same group kept growing and growing. We had almost the entire lunchroom area filled with friends and adopted family, as we called each other.

If we didn't know someone, it was because they were new to the group or school. It was everyone fits in or they don't sit in. We never really had that rule everyone was just left the same as everyone else. We had gay men and women, straight folks too, there were people of every nation practically, and we had white and black sitting together talking about the same things in what seemed like a peaceful resolution to a problem that other classes couldn't figure out.

It felt like I had a family for the very first time in my life. I had friends in a school where I was told that there were gang banging thugs and drugs going around the world inside of there and police to monitor the halls. We didn't see or hear any of it. We took our affections and our pride and threw it out the window and gave out love to those who needed it more. It was truly a family of people from all sorts of backgrounds, and we didn't care about our differences, and that was what helped us bring so many closer together.

All was peaceful until I started to act out on several other girls in the group. I was not a very pleasant person to sit next to if I was on a spree of horny antics. Girls hated when I would touch them, but I didn't care it was all fun to me. I wasn't trying to sex them up at this point, but I wanted to. In my mind my girlfriend was still seeing other men on the side at her high school, and so I was going to do the same since we were only friends at the time. That same action had a negative effect on the lunch group around us and it slowly dwindled away from the eighty plus people we usually had.

The only friend I ended up with at the end of a long and strenuous time of hurting was my cute little Latino friend who sat with me in the hallways. She was only close to me because I wouldn't leave her alone. I would bother everyone for affection and attention that I didn't get at home. Love seemed so hard for me to grasp onto. The people around me seemed to turn their lives away from helping me, and refused to go any further.

My mind started racing faster, and into a frame of mind of guilt and shame. My body took on most of the punishment for my stupidity and actions at that time. I wouldn't eat most of the time, and when I did eat it was too much for me to digest. I started wearing shirts with symbols of drug use on them, even though I hadn't smoked marijuana since the tenth grade I was gaining attention by wearing it even if it was bad attention I liked it. The world would be focused on my needs rather than their own needs and wants. Attention was awesome for me no matter if it was good attention or bad attention. It all felt the same when I received it. I felt accepted when I was receiving attention from my pears.

I didn't like feeling empty inside. I really didn't like feeling used by those who cared about me. Instead of letting others use me I used myself to get the attention and popularity that I felt I deserved and wanted.

I felt like the world should have to care now about my own thoughts and actions. I would have people doing my bidding at the end of the day. I wanted more people to control, and I wanted them to see how much I had changed. All of which was playing out in my mind, but I saw it as a reality.

I would talk bad about others, and they wouldn't even bat an eye. People seemed to becoming scared of what I might have done next. My anger would rage out like my brother's and my face would turn bright red. My eyes would turn red from the tension I emitted from my body. People said I looked like I had the devil in my body.

While I didn't think about killing myself, I did think about harming the world around me. The people who attempted to interfere with my plans were my targets. Mainly the targets would have been the popular kids and those who treated me like a subhuman doormat. I had never broken out into a fight in high school, but I did find myself tearing at the top of my lungs screaming for people to quit talking bad about the substitute teacher in the choir room. Then the class drew silent for a moment not expecting the problems to quietly settle down so quickly by one voice. I for one couldn't stand another person being mentally hurt by other people. Especially someone who I saw as a guest instructor while the real teacher was out on a medical leave of absence.

It felt good to release my aggression out on the others who were so rude to me or another person. I drew back some of the energy incase I had to fight with someone, but it never came down to it. I had most of my sanity left to deal with just about anyone I was angry at.

In my mind, I was thinking negative thoughts throughout my days at high school. Bullies would attempt to prove what they had to prove to their other bully friends, why they needed to be a bigger person than the last one. Those same bullies received a huge verbal assault from my arsenal of words and high volume toned speech. I took down many of the bullies with one word or two. Teachers would swarm the bully attempting to attack me physically, and I became excellent at it catching people off guard and tearing down their so call defenses. Plus I had friends in the crowd of people I was with that would back me up in any way possible. That meant even if they had to step in and help a little.

Students would make fun of my very large duffle bag until they saw what I was using the books inside for. It swung really well too. Add to the fight that if I were to get jumped I always had friends backing me up. It was never that ugly in my life though. Most of my violence happened at home with my brother.

Also at home I would have hours of pornography dubbed and thousands of pictures of pornographic images.

It was this type of thinking that caused me to have those hundreds of hours of pornography. My thinking seemed logically sound since I was always around the problem from my younger age to where I was then at age eighteen. I had a softer side for women who were being harassed in the halls of the high school. If a man walked by and wolf-called at a girl I was there to take him aside for the most part and let him know that it wasn't right doing it. But I knew I wasn't any better with my touching of the same women, but I liked it more!

I can't blame those people for my own actions, but I do blame them for showing me their negative behaviors. After all, it was my own actions that took a lot of my friends and made them pick sides for their fight against what I was doing to others.

Many of my friends were attempting to tell my girlfriend that I was a no good person, and that I would cheat on her at the flip of a hat. I was grateful that she didn't just listen to their words and actually took what I had to say to heart. I couldn't have asked for a better prayer to be answered than when my girlfriend continuously helped me to see what I was doing, and when she decided to help me to turn my life around. I owned her my life.

I jumped at a lot of dysfunctional opportunities over the years that nearly cost my relationship with everyone I had loved. I dreamt of the day that I could leave my parents house, but not because of my mother or father, but because of my haunted past in the dungeon of a bedroom that I dwelled in for so many years. My past kept coming back and haunting my present life until I faced my fears of it.

One thing that I was really ashamed about was that in the first twelve years of my life I had experienced more sexual relations than most people did in the lifetime. My life still wasn't changed from this type of behavior, not yet! I had a long ways to go to get the sobriety back and free myself from my addiction.

That senior year, I graduated, lettering in choir. I also managed to still make the final choir trip I would have taken with my friends from the choir to Branson, where I was again alone for the fourth straight year.

If you looked at my life back then you couldn't tell that I wasn't happy. My smiles always seemed to be genuine and from the heart. I guess I had some good people around me, because my smile wasn't always as bright as I was told it was. At least that was how I felt many days in those school years.

As I walked across that stage to grab my diploma from the staff, as they called out my name, I looked out over the crowds of people, and I could hear the choir in the back of the gymnasium shout out a huge yell for me. That's when it hit me that I was actually loved by those people; those years of hardships were not all in vein.

I wanted my childhood back, but I could never totally regain my virginity in my mind. I had always felt it was taken from me too soon. My childhood wasn't a childhood as much as it was a nightmare that wouldn't leave me alone. I know now that people couldn't even begin to understand why I acted the ways I did. And so I had to write it out for them to experience what I felt.

If you had to ask me what I missed out of my life the most, I would say that it was having a day I shared with someone who didn't seem to take advantage of my childlike will, or my soul. My soul was lost for a very long time but it wasn't dead, I let it lay dormant until it could fully heal from the past damages that were caused by others who didn't know or didn't see the pain they had bestowed into hurting my heart.

The addiction isn't really about love, sex, or any other part that I was having the problems with, but it was about control over my own actions, my feelings, and my words that I would say to other people. These were the only things I could have ever controlled, and it was feeling powerless over those ideas that made me feel helpless, hopeless, and alone.

In the end of the school year I knew what had to come next, college, marriage, children of my own, and a way of life that I would have to live and find out where it was that I was going to help lead all of that in a better direction that what I was lead down.

The damage had been done, and I couldn't allow this to hurt my life or my spirit any further. I hid it away until the time was right to come out about the entire thing. And what better way to do that then to tell you my story.

This story of my life was meant to be shared through God's will over me. I know there are those out there that don't believe in a form of God, that don't believe in religion, or don't believe in a higher power of sorts, but I encourage those of you who don't to pray for God's will to come down over you and whatever that means God will eventually show you. And for those people who still don't believe in a higher power after reading my story I just want to leave you all with this thought. Are you "Bigger Than Me?"

So while you ponder that question, I just want to tell everyone who reads this story of my life that while yes I blamed a lot of people for my problems, I had found a way to stop blaming others, and that too was through God's love for me. If it weren't for God's love over me, I would have already died a slow and painful death, and never understanding or sharing my story with the world, and possibly never making a difference to at least one soul who is in the same place as I was in their life at one point in time or another. And remember that God's love for you and I is always Bigger than Me!